Redemption

The Foundation of Worship

By
Dr. Michael Elliott

Vision Publishing · Ramona, California

Redemption: The Foundation of Worship

© Copyright 2004 by Michael Elliott

ISBN # 1-931178-75-5

All rights in this book are reserved worldwide. No part of the book may be reproduced in any manner, whatsoever, without written permission of the author except brief quotations embodied in critical articles or reviews.

Vision Publishing
1520 Main Street, Suite C
Ramona CA 92065
www.vision.edu/publishing
Printed in the United States of America

TABLE OF CONTENTS

Chapter One
    WORSHIP IS THE PURPOSE OF MAN 11

Chapter Two
    WORSHIP FLOWS OUT OF REDEMPTION 22

Chapter Three
    WORSHIP IS ROOTED IN DELIVERANCE 33

Chapter Four
    WORSHIP IN THE COVENANT LAW 38

Chapter Five
    WORSHIP IS THE MINISTRY OF THE PRIESTHOOD 43

Chapter Six
    WORSHIP PATTERNS IN THE TABERNACLE OF MOSES 55

Chapter Seven
    WORSHIP IS OUR RESPONSE TO KNOWING GOD 67

Chapter Eight
    WORSHIP REVEALED IN THE NAMES OF GOD 72

BIBLIOGRAPHY 83

PREFACE

Peeling back the curtains of time and eternity, we see that the chief activity of heaven is, and has always been, the worship of God. All the inhabitants of heaven gather around the throne to continually offer their praise and worship to the Lord.

Lucifer was the worship leader of heaven in eternity past, and the language of music was built within him. His responsibilities were to orchestrate the praise and worship of heaven. However, Lucifer's heart became lifted up in pride over his wisdom and beauty. Believing that it was he that should rule heaven and be worshiped, he led a rebellion against God. God judged Lucifer, and the angels who followed him, and cast them out of heaven.

After the rebellion of Lucifer, God was once again the sole object of heaven's worship. Yet, even with the full attention of the angels continually ministering before Him, God's heart was not fulfilled. He wanted more than what the angels were capable of giving Him. God wanted a family—a family that would respond to His overtures of love. He wanted a family that adored Him and not just appreciated His provision. God desired a family that would serve Him out of the desire of their hearts, and not the duty of their flesh. God longed for a family that would unashamedly, and openly, be expressive in their praise and worship of Him.

In God's divine counsel, He decided to create man. God destined man to fulfill two basic assignments in the earth. The first and foremost assignment was that man was to worship Him. The second assignment, which is directly tied to the first purpose of worship, is ruler-ship over God's creation. God intended for man to worship Him and to rule over the works of His hands.

God named the first man, Adam. Everything was just fine until Adam rebelled against God and violated the only restriction that God had placed on him. In that very moment, when Adam sinned against God, he died spiritually, and began to die physically. Adam's relationship, and his fellowship with God, was broken; for Adam's sin separated him from the presence of God. The purpose of man's worship and his ruler-ship had been thwarted by sin.

The tragedy of sin, and the resulting penalty of death, passed to all men. Every man that has ever been born has been born with Adam's fallen nature. God expelled Adam from the Garden of Eden because He was no longer able to fellowship with Adam, or to trust Him. Because of Adam's sin, the ground was cursed and the animal kingdom became filled with fear and hate.

God's heart was broken over His loss of Adam's fellowship and worship; therefore, God prophesied to the serpent who had beguiled Eve, Adam's wife. God prophesied that one day a Redeemer would come and put an end to Lucifer's kingdom. This promised Redeemer would be born of the seed of a woman and would redeem mankind from sin.

God would not give up on man, His highest creation. God pursued man with love, and established a way for man to come before Him and be restored to a right relationship with God. Once restored in his relationship with God, he could again be restored to his purpose of ruler-ship in the earth.

The way of approach to God was established by God, Himself. Only through the blood of the sacrifice could man approach God, be forgiven, and cleansed from his sins. It was God, Who provided the first sacrifice for sin in the Garden of Eden for Adam and Eve. This pattern was to be taught to all future generations as the only acceptable way of approach to God. The blood sacrifice was also the only means of expressing worship to God.

The nation of Israel had turned away from God and failed to keep the conditions of their covenant relationship with God. As a result, they were in Egypt and found themselves in bondage to Pharaoh. Israel cried out to God for deliverance. God heard their cries, and sent Moses to lead them out of slavery in Egypt.

The issue of worship was at the root of Israel's deliverance from Egypt. Pharaoh challenged God for the worship and service of the Israelites. God protected the Israelites from the various plagues that He perpetrated on the Egyptians. The blood of the sacrificial lamb became Israel's protection from the last and final plague; that being, death.

After crossing the Red Sea, and watching God defeat Pharaoh and his army, the Israelites began to rejoice and offer their praise to God. Every time that God redeemed Israel from the hand of the enemy, worship flowed out of their hearts to God in praise for His redeeming work. Redemption is the foundation of worship: worship is to flow out of redemption.

God commanded Moses to build the Tabernacle of Moses in order to provide a place for Him to continually dwell with His people. It is through the Tabernacle of Moses that we can clearly see the patterns of worship and approach to God.

The Mosaic economy was built on foundational truths and each point us to Christ and His ministry to us, and through us. These truths establish for us the patterns which we approach God, as we come before Him to worship. The patterns for worship, as set forth in the Mosaic economy, do not merely restrict us to the rituals of worship, but rather, they release the inspiration we need in order to understand Who we worship, and why.

The Tabernacle of Moses only functioned around, and on the basis of, the blood sacrifice. Apart from the blood of the sacrifice, man could not approach God. Because of sin, man lost his understanding of God's great love and desire for him; therefore, he lost his understanding of his purpose in the earth. God knew that unless man restored his knowledge of God, he would never be restored to relationship with God; therefore, he would never be restored to his purpose in the earth.

God set His heart to reveal Himself to mankind. Through His glorious creation, God made Himself known to man. God also chose to reveal Himself through His redemptive names. These revelations of God were progressive in nature, and with each revelation of Himself, God would wait for Israel to begin to walk in the light of that particular revelation before revealing more of Himself to them. Actually, in this progressive revelation, the great mercy of God was seen. The revelation of God's redemptive names was so overwhelming, that it took time for Israel to understand and embrace each particular aspect of God.

God believed that if we ever really got to know Him, in all of His love and power, then we would love and worship Him only. All He wants us to do is consider His gift of salvation and His offer of eternal life. Once we see Him as He really is, and consider His gifts to us, we will worship Him. Just as redemption was the basis of

Israel's worship, even so today, redemption must be the foundation of our worship.

Chapter One

WORSHIP IS THE PURPOSE OF MAN

The Bible proclaims that we were created for the pleasure of God. Upon this premise, we must seek an answer to the following question: "What are the activities and the attitudes of man that will fulfill the heart of God and bring Him pleasure?" In order to fully understand what brings God pleasure, we must lift the veil of time and look into eternity past. There, in eternity past, we understand that which brings God pleasure.

The chief activity of heaven always has been, and forever shall be, the praise and worship of God. The sound that permeates and dominates the air of heaven is the praise and worship of God. Throughout all of eternity, the inhabitants of heaven have ministered to the Lord before His throne in expressions of praise and worship.

The excellent works of God's hands are celebrated through praise. However, through worship, we acknowledge God's worthiness. The continual revelation of God's attributes, His nature, and His character, inspire worship in the heart of the worshiper. Without ceasing, praise and worship ascends to the throne of God from the four living creatures and the twenty-four elders as found in Revelation 4:8-11:

> *"The four living creatures, each having six wings, were full of eyes around and within. And they do not rest day or night, saying: 'Holy, holy, holy, Lord God Almighty, Who was and is and is to come!' Whenever the living creatures give glory and honor and thanks to Him who sits on the throne, who lives forever and ever, the twenty-four elders fall down before Him who sits on the throne and worship Him who lives forever and ever, and cast their crowns before the throne, saying: 'You are worthy, O Lord, to receive glory and honor and power; for You created all things, and by Your will they exist and were created.'"*

The assignment given to the angels is that of praise and worship. *"When He again brings the firstborn into the world, He says: 'Let all the angels of God worship Him'"* (Hebrews 1:6). We can clearly see, from the activity of the inhabitants of heaven who gather around the throne of God, that it is praise and worship that will please and fulfill the heart of God.

The worship leader of heaven was the archangel, Lucifer. He was God's most prized creation among all of the inhabitants of heaven. Lucifer was a picture of perfection for he was full of beauty and wisdom. *"Son of man, take up a lamentation for the king of Tyre, and say to him, 'Thus says the Lord God: "You were the seal of perfection, full of wisdom and perfect in beauty"'"* (Ezekiel 28:12).

God created Lucifer with music in his very being; and he spoke with music which was the glorious language of praise and worship. Therefore, Lucifer fully understood the power of melodies, harmonies, and rhythms. All of the inhabitants of heaven responded to his passionate leadership, as he orchestrated heaven's worship of God.

Lucifer, which was called "the anointed cherub who covers," was the closest to God's throne out of all of God's creation. His assignment was not only to lead the praise and worship in heaven, but he was also to guard the very throne of God. For this most important task of guardianship, Lucifer was anointed with God's authority. Lucifer was so close to God, that he freely walked the mountain of God amidst the fire of God's holiness. *"You were the anointed cherub who covers; I established you; you were on the holy mountain of God; you walked back and forth in the midst of fiery stones"* (Ezekiel 28:14).

With all of his beauty and perfection, one would assume that Lucifer would guard his heart in order to stay humble before God, his Creator. However, he did not guard his heart, and his heart became lifted up with pride because of his wisdom and beauty. When his heart became corrupted with pride, the seed of rebellion was planted. Lucifer considered how beautiful and how wise he really was, and he began to covet the praise and the worship that belonged to God. He not only desired to be worshiped, but he also wanted to take God's place on the throne and rule all of heaven.

Lucifer turned his focus from the beauty of God's holiness to exalt his own beauty and wisdom. The desire of his heart was no longer to lead the worship of heaven; now he wanted to become the object of heaven's worship. *"For you have said in your heart: 'I will ascend into heaven, I will exalt my throne above the stars of God; I will also sit on the mount of the congregation on the farthest sides of the north; I will ascend above the heights of the clouds, I will be like the Most High'"* (Isaiah 14:13-14).

There were two issues which inflamed the heart of Lucifer and these issues incited him to rebel against God. The first issue was that he wanted to be worshiped. The second issue was that he wanted to gain absolute power and authority over God's creation by overthrowing God and use his power to exercise dominion over the works of God's hands.

Lucifer perverted the authority that had been given to him to guard the holiness of God. He prostituted this God-given authority by leading a rebellion against God, among the angels. *"Your heart was lifted up because of your beauty; you corrupted your wisdom for the sake of your splendor"* (Ezekiel 28:17). Nearly one-third of the angels became participants in Lucifer's rebellion and followed him in his sin against God.

God would not tolerate Lucifer's, or the angel's, sin of rebellion against Him. God pronounced His judgment against Lucifer, promising that He would destroy him. *"By the abundance of your trading you became filled with violence within, and you sinned; Therefore I cast you as a profane thing out of the mountain of God; and I destroyed you, O covering cherub, from the midst of the fiery stones"* (Ezekiel 28:16). The judgment of God began as Lucifer and his band of rebel angels were forever cast out of heaven. *"How you are fallen from heaven, O Lucifer, son of the morning! How you are cut down to the ground, you who weakened the nations"* (Isaiah 14:12)!

The rebellion, and ensuing battle, interrupted the flow of worship in heaven for a season. The attention that was to be showered on God, in praise and worship, was redirected toward putting down the rebellion of Lucifer and his followers—this deeply grieved the heart of God. The pleasure that God received, from being the sole object of praise and worship, was spoiled; thus, the heart of God was not fulfilled.

The rebellion of Lucifer faded in the light of God's glory and Heaven soon resounded with praise and worship again. God was restored to His rightful place as the sole object of the affection and worship of the inhabitants of heaven. Yet, even with the full attention and worship of the angels, God's heart was not satisfied nor fulfilled. He wanted something more than what the angels were capable of giving Him. He longed for fellowship on a higher level than that which He received from the angels.

God wanted a family. This family would consist of a creation that was higher than the angels. He wanted a family who would be completely devoted to Him and Him alone. He wanted a family who would be responsive to His love. He wanted a family who would be expressive in praise and worship. And lastly, He wanted a family from whom worship would flow out of a heart full of desire for Him. God would grant His new family full authority to rule and exercise dominion over the works of His hands.

In the divine counsel of God, He decided to create man. When God created the beasts of the field, He patterned them one after the other. When He created the birds of the air, He patterned them, likewise, one after the other. However, when it came to man God decided to create man in His own image and likeness.

> *"Then God said, 'Let Us make man in Our image, according to Our likeness; let them have dominion over the fish of the sea, over the birds of the air, and over the cattle, over all the earth and over every creeping thing that creeps on the earth.' So God created man in His own image; in the image of God He created him; male and female He created them. Then God blessed them, and God said to them, 'Be fruitful and multiply; fill the earth and subdue it; have dominion over the fish of the sea, over the birds of the air, and over every living thing that moves on the earth'"* (Genesis 1:26-28).

God destined man for two basic assignments in the earth. These two assignments are tied together, for each assignment flows out of the other. The first assignment God relegated to man was for man to worship Him; God created man to be a worshiper. The need and the desire to worship a supreme-being is built into every heart. God always intended for that supreme-being to be Himself. Man was to fulfill his responsibility of worshiping God by daily fellowshipping with Him. Therefore, worship becomes the natural response of companionship.

The Bible clearly mandates that all of God's creation was, and is to be, a statement of praise to Him. This celebration of praise was to be led by man. The Psalmist David said, *"Let every thing that has breath praise the Lord. Praise the Lord"* (Psalms 150:6). The Apostle Paul stated, *"That we should be to the praise of His glory, who first trusted in Christ"* (Ephesians 1:12). The Apostle John declared, *"Thou art worthy, O Lord, to receive glory and honor and power: for Thou hast created all things, and for Thy pleasure they are and were created"* (Revelation 4:11).

The second assignment relegated to man in the earth, was that man would have dominion over all of the works of God's hands. Man was to fulfill his responsibility of ruler-ship by simply exercising his God-given authority over the works of God's hands.

> *"Man is by nature religious. He was created to worship. If he does not worship the true and living God, by the power of the Holy Spirit, then he often resorts to the counterfeit, accepting another form of religion and worshiping the god of this world, with the help of evil spirits."*[1]

The earth was God's gift to man. God prepared the earth not only for man to dwell on, but to have dominion over. *"The heaven, even the heaven, are the Lord's: but the earth hath He given to the children of men"* (Psalms 115:16). God stored treasures within the earth for man to find and use; treasures that would enrich man's life.

---

[1]*The Foundations of Christian Doctrine*, Copyright 1980 by Kevin J. Conner, Bible Temple Publications.

Just beneath the crust of the earth, God implanted precious gems; and He laced the mountains with silver and gold, along with other important ores. God planted lush, tropical gardens and giant forests. God molded man's earth with majestic mountain ranges and peaceful valleys. The animal kingdom was created for companionship, as well as, for man's food and clothing.

The sum total of God's creation was for the pleasure and the benefit of man; for man, is the crown of God's creation and he is God's greatest and highest work. The Psalmist David pondered the work of God in creating man, and wondered why man was so special to God. He wondered why God favored man so, and paid so much attention to man. He especially wondered why God gave man authority to rule over God's great creation.

> *"When I consider Your heavens, the work of Your fingers, the moon and the stars, which You have ordained, what is man that You are mindful of him, and the son of man that You visit him? For You have made him a little lower than the angels, and You have crowned him with glory and honor. You have made him to have dominion over the works of Your hands; You have put all things under his feet"* (Psalms 8:3-6).

Adam, being the first man on the earth, became the most prolific worshiper of God the earth has ever known. Adam was privileged to worship God from the vantage point of sinlessness. Adam's fellowship with God was not poisoned with sin; therefore, he completely knew God. He enjoyed a daily fellowship with God that was founded on perfect love, perfect trust, and perfect communication. Praise and worship flowed from Adam to God as naturally, and as freely, as a river flows towards the sea. Without effort, Adam loved, served, and worshiped his friend and creator—God.

We can see in Adam, God's purpose for man in the earth. Man was created to worship God and take dominion over the works of God's hands. Man's worship and ruler-ship should be based on a love relationship with God that is founded on trust and desire. These two powerful streams are to flow out of man without effort.

Man is to serve God from the desire of his heart, not the duty of his flesh. Only when man responds to God from the desire of his heart will his worship please, and fulfill, the heart of God. Consequently, only when man responds to God from the desire of his heart will his ruler-ship be effective in the earth.

God gave Adam only one restriction when He placed him in the Garden of Eden. Adam's obedience in adhering to this restriction was mandatory to Adam's relationship with God. God was so serious about this one restriction, that He warned Adam if he failed in obedience, and broke the restriction, it would cost Adam his life. Therefore, Adam could not afford to fail or he would die physically, as well as, spiritually. *"And the Lord God commanded the man, saying, 'Of every tree of the Garden you may freely eat; but of the tree of the knowledge of good and evil you shall not eat, for in the day that you eat of it you shall surely die'"* (Genesis 2:16-17).

Eve was deceived by the serpent, and she picked the fruit from the forbidden tree. The moment that Eve ate of the fruit, she sinned against God. Eve then offered the fruit to Adam. Adam took the forbidden fruit from Eve and ate it, and in doing so, he failed to keep the one restriction that God had placed on him. Adam was not deceived as Eve had been; he knew exactly what he was doing in eating the forbidden fruit. He willfully rebelled against God's command. Adam became a sinner in that moment because he chose against God. *"Adam was not deceived, but the woman being deceived, fell into transgression"* (I Timothy 2:14).

Adam's sin had ensuing results; it not only devastated Adam, but has had an equally devastating affect on the whole human race. Personally, Adam's sin cost him his life; for the moment Adam sinned, he died spiritually and began to die physically. His wonderful fellowship and relationship with God was broken, for Adam's sin separated him from God. He yielded his authority to rule and have dominion over the works of God's hands to the devil. Even when Satan tempted Jesus in the wilderness, offering to Him all the kingdoms of the earth and their glory, Jesus did not deny that they were Satan's to offer. *"Again, the devil took Him up on an exceedingly high mountain, and showed Him all the kingdoms of the world and their glory. And he said to Him, 'All these things I will give You if You will fall down and worship me'"* (Matthew 4:8-9).

Adam's relationship with God, which was based on his love for God, was also broken; and his love for God was replaced by his fear of God. One of the saddest stories ever recorded was that, after Adam and Eve had sinned, they heard God walking in the Garden, and in fear, they hid themselves from Him.

Adam's rebellion against God brought a curse on the ground as well; even the plant kingdom was affected by Adam's sin. The ground now produced thorns and thistles instead of remaining in the perfected state as was found in the Garden of Eden.

> *"Then to Adam He said, 'Because you have heeded the voice of your wife, and have eaten from the tree of which I commanded you, saying, 'You shall not eat of it': Cursed is the ground for your sake; in toil you shall eat of it all the days of your life. Both thorns and thistles it shall bring forth for you, and you shall eat the herb of the field'"* (Genesis 3:17-18).

Adam's sin also reached into the animal kingdom. Prior to the entrance of sin into the world, all of the animals lived in perfect peace and harmony. However, after Adam's fall, the peace, harmony, and love that governed the animal kingdom was replaced with fear and hate. Where the lion and the lamb once frolicked together; now the lamb had become the prey of the lion.

The most devastating aspect of Adam's rebellion against God, was to be realized in the far-reaching effect sin would have on the human race. All men have become partakers of Adam's sin, for his fallen nature has passed to all men. Adam is the natural father of the human race; therefore, the seed of rebellion has been planted in the hearts of all men in every generation and produces the fruit of sin in mankind.

Just as in Adam all men are made sinners, also in Adam, all men are placed under the condemning sentence of death: *"For all have sinned, and come short of the glory of God"* (Romans 3:23); *"For the wages of sin is death"* (Romans 6:23); *"Wherefore, as by one man sin entered into the world, and death by sin; and so death passed upon all men, for that all have sinned"* (Romans 5:12).

Mankind was not only made sinners and sentenced to die for their sins, but they were under the full weight of condemnation for their sins. *"He who believes in Him is not condemned; but he who does not believe is condemned already, because he has not believed in the name of the only begotten Son of God"* (John 3:18). Just as the trespass of Adam produced death in Adam, even so, the trespasses of men produce death before God. The Book of Ephesians tells us that man is reckoned as dead, *"And you hath He quickened, who were dead in trespasses and sins"* (Ephesians 2:1).

The nature of man is at war with God for there is nothing in the heart, or the flesh of man, that is favorable towards God. Man's nature will always be at war against the ways of the Lord. *"Because the carnal mind is enmity against God; for it is not subject to the law of God, nor indeed can be"* (Romans 8:7).

Hope is very important to mankind for if a man's hope is shattered or gone, his heart will sink in despair. Due to Adam's sin, all hope was gone. Literally, man was living in a world separated from God; therefore, totally without hope. *"That at that time you were without Christ, being aliens from the commonwealth of Israel and strangers from the covenants of promise, having no hope and without God in the world"* (Ephesians 2:12).

Adam yielded his right and authority to rule over God's creation. Now, not only was Adam's dominion gone, but he was also subject to the power of the devil. This fallen nature of man is under the influence of the devil and has become subject to all of his desires and schemes.

Jesus told the disciples that the devil desired to steal from mankind, to kill mankind, and even to destroy mankind. Paul points out that man, apart from Christ, lives his life according to his fallen and base nature; and this nature is under the influence of the devil. *"In which you once walked according to the course of this world, according to the prince of the power of the air, the spirit who now works in the sons of disobedience"* (Ephesians 2:2).

Not only did man find himself under the influence of the devil, but he discovered that he was living under a curse of failure because of Adam's sin. Man was destined to a live a life of failure in every arena: failure in finances; failure in marriage and family relationships; failure in health; and worst of all, the ultimate failure—death. All of man's successes that were gained were canceled under this curse. The successes were given over to the ultimate failure—death. Man, even in his best attempts to serve God, was destined to failure. *"For as many as are of the works of the law are under the curse; for it is written, 'Cursed is everyone who does not continue in all things which are written in the Book of the Law, to do them'"* (Galatians 3:10).

Man was spiritually blinded by Adam's sin and could no longer see the beauty of God and the value of His truth. Man, in his own estimation, had a better way of living than the way that God had prescribed. *"Whose minds the god of this age has blinded, who do not believe, lest the light of the Gospel of the glory of Christ, who is the image of God, should shine on them"* (II Corinthians 4:4).

One of the most devastating effects of Adam's sin was evidenced in the hardened heart of fallen mankind. In the very beginning, the heart of man was soft and responsive to God and His desires; but now, due to sin, man's heart was hardened to the needs of God's heart. He could no longer feel the love of God or even respond to God in love. Man's heart became wicked and deceitful, instead of being loving and full of integrity, as found in John 12:40, *"He hath blinded their eyes, and hardened their heart."*

Adam grieved over what he had done; he realized that he had failed God. Not only had he failed God, but now, God was rejecting him. God would not, and could not, fellowship with him like they had fellowshipped just one day before he had sinned. Weighed down with guilt, Adam was driven out of his Garden home. Not only was Adam driven from his home, he was driven out of the very presence of God.

The realization struck him that he was not only rejected by God, but that God no longer trusted him. Adam was well aware of the cherubim with the flaming sword that God had placed in the Garden. These cherubim were to not only protect the tree of life, but they were to deny Adam's re-entrance into the Garden.

> *"Then the Lord God said, 'Behold, the man has become like one of Us, to know good and evil. And now, lest he put out his hand and take also of the tree of life, and eat, and live forever'— therefore the Lord God sent him out of the Garden of Eden to till the ground from which he was taken. So He drove out the man; and He placed cherubim at the east of the Garden of Eden, and a flaming sword which turned every way, to guard the way to the tree of life"* (Genesis 3:22-24).

No one will ever be able to grasp the depths of grief that God experienced when Adam rebelled. God's heart was broken as Adam knowingly, and willfully, chose against Him. God grieved because His relationship with Adam was broken. He grieved over Adam's spiritual death, and over the corruption that had permeated Adam's flesh; for God knew this would cause him to die physically as well.

God grieved because the worship that He had received, through Adam's fellowship, would cease. It grieved God's heart to know, that because of His righteous nature, He would have to bring judgment on Adam and subsequently, on all mankind. God grieved as He knew the judgment on fallen mankind, was death.

God grieved over the lost fellowship with Adam, for Adam was His friend. Forever gone were the tender words of love expressed to each other as they greeted the dawn of each new day. Forever gone was the laughter He shared with Adam as they talked in the warm afternoon sun. Forever gone were the quiet moments of solitude that they shared as they strolled together in the cool breeze of the evening. Forever gone was the comfort received from songs they sang under His diamond-studded heavens.

Again, God's heart was broken as He drove Adam and Eve out of the Garden that He had lovingly prepared for them. As much as God wanted to reach out and overlook Adam's sin, He knew that He couldn't. His righteousness would neither allow sin, nor the sinner, to be in His presence. He knew that He could not embrace man as a sinner, because the fire of His holiness would consume a sinful man.

God had to provide another way for Adam, and fallen mankind, to fellowship with Him again.

Chapter Two

WORSHIP FLOWS OUT OF REDEMPTION

Once again, God was overwhelmed and consumed with His loneliness. Out of a broken and grieving heart, a seething river of anger arose in God. God prophesied the birth of a Redeemer for mankind; this Redeemer would be the virgin-born seed of a woman. This Redeemer would pay the price that would be required to redeem mankind from the bondage of sin; thereby, delivering him from the kingdom of darkness. This wonderful Redeemer of man would one day render the enemies of God powerless, and destroy the works of the devil's kingdom, once and for all. *"And I will put enmity between you and the woman, and between your seed and her Seed; He shall bruise your head, and you shall bruise His heel"* (Genesis 3:15).

God was determined to redeem and restore His relationship, and His fellowship, with man. It was God, the offended party, who reached out first in an unfathomable expression of love and mercy to Adam; for Adam was hopelessly lost in his sin and forever separated from his God.

God set the pattern of approach for man to come again into His presence when He provided the first sacrifice for the atonement of Adam's sin. Man's redemption from sin was provided through the shed blood of an acceptable sacrifice; therein, the restoration of his relationship and fellowship with God was secured.

Sin demanded the death of the sinner; for the sins of man could be remitted only through a substitute death, and by the shedding of innocent blood. Death by any other means would not, and could not, propitiate man's sin. Innocent blood of a sacrifice was required because the life was in the blood. Blood is the only agent that will purge man of his sin, cleanse his conscience, and lift his burden of guilt. *"And according to the law almost all things are purified with blood, and without shedding of blood there is no remission"* (Hebrews 9:22).

The blood sacrifice was not just a means of approach into the presence of God—it was the only acceptable means of approach into

His presence. The blood sacrifice was not just a way to restore man's relationship and fellowship with God—it was the only way. God set the pattern of approach and that was through the shed blood of an innocent sacrifice. God would honor no other way of approach—it was His way, or no way.

God carefully instructed Adam concerning the proper way to approach Him and come into His presence. God taught Adam that the only way their relationship and their fellowship could be restored, was through the blood sacrifice. Adam learned from God the terrible price that must be paid for his sin; in that, only through the blood sacrifice could his sins be forgiven. God revealed to Adam that all of his expressions of worship would find their beginning at the altar of sacrifice. Adam learned that only through the blood sacrifice could his purpose of worship and ruler-ship in the earth be recovered. The blood sacrifice becomes the eternal pattern for worship, in that worship, is the natural outflow of redemption.

Adam not only adhered to this pattern of worship, personally, but he also taught it to his two sons, Cain and Abel. He instructed them in the way of approach into God's presence as He taught them to worship God through the blood sacrifice. No doubt, from the time of their youth, Cain and Abel watched, and perhaps even helped, their father present sacrifices of blood before the Lord. They stood by and observed their father as he worshiped the Lord from the place of sacrifice. Though it was not a pleasant sight, there was a sense of fulfillment as they heard their father offer thanks to the Lord for His love, mercy, and provision in their lives.

As a young adult, Cain worked in the fields planting and caring for his crops. There was a measure of pride in his heart as he gathered in the bountiful harvest. One day he came to the altar, where he had stood so many times before with his father, as they offered sacrifices to the Lord. Cain presented the produce from his harvest on the altar of worship with pride. Even though his offering was not according to the pattern that God had established, or that which his father had labored to teach him, he was confident that God would accept his offering and find pleasure in his worship.

God not only rejected Cain's offering, but God also rejected Cain. Cain had violated the pattern of redemption and worship. He ignored God's prescribed way of approach and came before God his own way. He failed in his worship because he presented God an offering that was the fruit of his labor and the produce of the ground (which was cursed because of sin). Regardless of how sincere his expression of worship was in his heart, there was no letting of blood; and thus, no remission of his sins. Therefore, God had no choice but to reject the worship and reject the worshiper because He had not come in the prescribed approach. *"And in the process of time it came to pass that Cain brought an offering of the fruit of the ground to the Lord, but He did not respect Cain and his offering. And Cain was very angry, and his countenance fell"* (Genesis 4:3, 5).

God's rejection of Cain's offering stands as a signpost to all of mankind that the only acceptable way of approach to God is through the blood of the sacrifice. We also learn that there is nothing of man, even in man's very best form and presentation, which is an acceptable way of approach into God's presence.

Abel, on the other hand, understood the pattern of worship by the blood sacrifice. He understood it was the only acceptable means of approach to God. He presented, on the altar of worship, a sacrificial offering which he had selected from the very best of his flock. As the smoke ascended from the altar, God was pleased with Abel's sacrifice and He accepted his expression of worship.

God's acceptance of Abel's offering stands as a signpost to all of mankind that the only acceptable way to approach God is by the blood of the sacrifice. We learn that we must come before God, not with the labor of our flesh, but with the obedience of our hearts. Since there is nothing of our flesh that is acceptable to God, we must throw ourselves on the mercy of God in our offerings and expressions of worship.

God could have exercised His omnipotent power to redeem man. God could have spoken a word and recovered all that had been lost in Adam's fall. Instead, God chose to quietly institute an act of worship through the rite of the blood sacrifice; for God knew a secret. He knew that obedient worship, as expressed in the blood sacrifice, would cleanse man of sin and would release His power in, and through, the worshiper. This obedient worship would bring about restoration and recover all that had been lost in Adam's fall. Only through the obedience and the worship of the blood sacrifice could man's relationship to God be restored, and his dominion over the works of God's hands be recovered.

This secret of obedient worship still applies to us today. Obedience restores our relationship to God and, therefore, releases our ruler-ship in the earth.

> *"As in the beginning when the foundations for man's life—his purpose and fulfillment were laid in worship, so redemption's program seeks to reinstate man by restoring those foundations. Though they have been crumbled by man's fall, Jesus Himself has established a new beginning point for perfect worship. He is the Sacrifice. He is the High Priest. He is the Leader in worship—restoring any member of Adam's race who will return to relationship with God. But restored relationship through reestablished worship is not the sum of the redemption plan. The full scope of the divine program of retrieval must not be narrowed. Man's restored relationship with God is intended to restore his ruler-ship as well. Repentance is in essence the renewal of worship. Because repentance resubmits us to God's rule again, two lost possibilities reappear: the resurrection of our relationship with Him and the restoration of our ruler-ship under Him. Our return to our place of obedient worship not only places us under God's kingdom rule again, it thereby makes possible a reinvestment of that rule among humankind."*[2]

Through the blood sacrifice, man not only received forgiveness of his sins, but he released the power of God to break sin's dominion over his life. God's power was realized in the worshiper with each act of obedience and with every expression of worship. This principle still applies today.

Long before the foundations of the world were laid, God had

---

[2]*Worship His Majesty.* Copyright 1987 by Jack Hayford, Word Publishing.

settled in His heart that the plan for man's redemption would be by means of the blood sacrifice. God knew, and therefore He purposed, that the only One qualified to fulfill the pattern and become the sacrifice for man's sin was His only Son, Jesus. Out of a heart full of love for man God presented, on the altar of worship, His own offering in the person of His Son. Jesus would be the ultimate and final blood sacrifice that would, once and for all, pay the penalty for man's transgressions. This final sacrifice would cleanse man of all unrighteousness.

In the fullness of time, Jesus was born of a virgin just as God had promised. Through His teachings and His miracles, Jesus revealed to mankind what the heart of God was like; and He showed to man how much God loved and cared for him. Jesus revealed to man the depth of God's desire for his fellowship and worship.

The days of His ministry drew to a close and Jesus knew that Calvary loomed on the horizon. In the still of the night, Jesus wrestled with His decision to become the ultimate sacrifice for the sins of mankind. He dreaded the excruciating physical pain that he would suffer as He was crucified. He dreaded the humiliation he would have to endure, as well as, the mockery of His name that He would be subjected to.

But most of all, He dreaded becoming soiled and stained with the vile sins of mankind. He knew full well that in becoming sin, His Father would turn away and abandon Him. Never had His fellowship been broken with His Father; and never had He been touched in the least way by sin. Now He was faced with becoming sin, and paying the penalty for man's sin in the shedding of His blood and His death on the Cross.

Jesus asked His Father if there was any other way that man could be redeemed. The Father replied that there was no other way for man to be redeemed from sin. Jesus understood that if He didn't submit Himself to the will of His Father, all of mankind would be eternally lost. Therefore, Jesus said "yes" to the Father's will and purpose for His life.

As the religious leaders were offering their lambs on the altar for sacrifice in the temple courtyard; God the Father carried His Lamb up a lonely hill, just outside the city gates. At Calvary, He presented

His Son, the Lamb of God, on the altar of the Cross. With His life, Jesus would pay the ultimate sacrifice for the sins of all mankind. God the Father knew that the sacrifice of His Son, and the shedding of His innocent blood, would once, and for all times, stay the hand of His judgment against the sins of any man who would cling to the Cross. Now through the death of Jesus, all men can be forgiven of their sins. All men can be saved from the wrath of God's judgment against sin, by simply appropriating Christ's death as the payment for their sins.

As Jesus hung on the Cross, His blood poured out of every wound that had been inflicted on Him. As His blood ran down His body and dripped into the dusty ground below, a stream of redemption and restoration began to flow to all of mankind. In the stream of His blood, everything that was lost in Adam's fall was restored to man. Jesus restored man's relationship to God through His payment for the sins that separated man from God. Now all men, who would come to the Cross, would not only be forgiven, but they would have the right to become the sons of God. *"But as many as received Him, to them gave He power to become the sons of God, even to them that believe on His name"* (John 1:12).

Jesus restored the gift of eternal life to mankind. Anyone who would believe on Jesus would receive the gift of eternal life; therefore, they would never be lost or perish. *"For God so loved the world that He gave His only begotten Son, that whosoever believeth in Him should not perish, but have everlasting life"* (John 3:16).

Jesus recovered man's authority to rule in the earth for Adam had given this authority to the devil in the Garden of Eden. Jesus openly spoiled principalities and the powers of the devil; and He gave to man His authority and power to exercise over the devil. *"For if by the one man's offense death reigned through the one, much more those who receive abundance of grace and of the gift of righteousness will reign in life through the One, Jesus Christ"* (Romans 5:17).

Jesus redeemed man from the penalty, the power, and the pollution of sin. Through His shed blood, sin has no right or power over the believer's life or body; and we are free from the power of sin. *"He has delivered us from the power of darkness and conveyed us into the kingdom of the Son of His love, in whom we have redemption through His blood, the forgiveness of sins"* (Colossians 1:13-14).

Jesus redeemed man's life from the destruction of God's wrath and judgment of sin. Jesus accomplished this by suffering the fullness of God's wrath and judgment for us on the Cross. Now, instead of judgment, we receive mercy. *"Who redeems your life from destruction, Who crowns you with loving-kindness and tender mercies"* (Psalms 103:4).

Jesus redeemed man from the curse of failure by becoming a curse for man on the Cross. Now, in Christ, man does not have to fail in any arena of his life. Jesus is our total victory. *"Christ has redeemed us from the curse of the law, having become a curse for us (for it is written, 'Cursed is everyone who hangs on a tree')"* (Galatians 3:13).

Jesus redeemed man from the works of the devil through His death on the Cross and His triumphant resurrection from the dead. Now, that which the devil works in our lives for our harm, Jesus turns for our good because we love Him. *"The thief does not come except to steal, and to kill, and to destroy. I have come that they may have life, and that they may have it more abundantly"* (John 10:10).

Redemption was birthed out of the loving heart of God the Father and was manifested in the ultimate obedience of His only Begotten Son, Jesus—even obedience unto death. God forever proved to the world that He truly loved mankind by giving His greatest gift, and most costly sacrifice. Because of His love for us, He gave Jesus as the payment for man's sin and the sole provision for man's salvation. The Apostle Paul stated, *"But God demonstrates His own love toward us, in that while we were still sinners, Christ died for us"* (Romans 5:8).

To prove His deep love and desire for man, God responded first to man. Jesus said that the love of God, expressed on the Cross, was the greatest manifestation of love the world had ever seen, or will ever experience. *"Greater love hath no man than this, that a man lay down his life for his friends"* (John 15:13).

Birthed in God's love for man, redemption becomes the very foundation for man's worship. All man needs to do is stop and consider the great love of God as expressed at Calvary; wherein, the natural response of man will be worship from a heart of gratitude.

Today, the issues which surround Satan's challenges to believers are the same as they were in eternity past, and to Adam in the Garden. Satan still wants to take God's place on the throne of our hearts and exercise dominion over every arena of our lives. Satan still seeks the worship of our hearts; therefore, he vies for our attention each day. He interprets our complaints concerning our circumstances, as praises of his work against us.

It is only through Christ that man can successfully address the challenges of Satan. Jesus gave us His full armor so that we can withstand the attacks of the enemy. He has vested His authority in us; therefore, we have power over the devil and his work in our lives. The Word teaches us that we are to completely submit ourselves to God, and resist the devil; wherein, we will stand victorious in Christ.

Man's worship of God, and his ruler-ship over the works of God's hands, are the two highest callings of God to man. Only when man can fully understand the Father's desire for worship, and wherein worship is rooted, can he fulfill his purpose in the earth.

There are many wonderful definitions of worship that have been given over the years as we have tried to understand what God desires. Each definition paints a beautiful picture as to one or more aspects of worship. In an attempt to sum up all of the various definitions of worship, we could say that worship is simply, yet profoundly, love responding to love.

Our worship is born out of a relationship with God and is based on the redemptive work of Christ. Our worship is daily nourished as we respond to God's presence and His abundant expressions of love. Our worship is preserved by the obedience of our hearts when we fully embrace the Word and the ways of the Lord.

The great price that Jesus paid to redeem us from sin restores our relationship to God. Our natural response to this gift should flow from a heart of gratitude, as expressed in worship. As we submit our hearts to the Lord and spend time in His presence, our love for Him, and our understanding of what pleases Him in our expressions of worship, will grow.

Just as God planned for man to be a worshiper, whose worship is rooted and founded in redemption, so redemption becomes the theme of God's desired pattern for man's worship.

Perhaps the clearest picture of God's established pattern for worship is seen in Israel's deliverance from the bondage of Egypt. It is during this period of Israel's history, that God began to reveal Himself through His redemptive names.

His revelation of Himself would establish the pattern for worship in their lives. God's desire for Israel was for them to become a nation of priests that would minister to Him from the redemptive posture of the blood sacrifice. This priestly ministry was to be performed according to the pattern set forth in the Tabernacle of Moses.

God commissioned Moses to build a place for Him to dwell with His people; this dwelling place was called the Tabernacle of Moses. The word tabernacle simply means, "to dwell with;" thus, the purpose of the Tabernacle was to provide God a place to be close to His people.

The blood sacrifice would be the basis of Israel's approach and fellowship with the Lord. Israel's sins could not be forgiven, or their burden of guilt lifted, by any other means than by the blood of the sacrifice. Their prayers to the Lord would not be heard, or their worship of the Lord received, unless they presented the blood of the sacrifice as an offering to the Lord. Everything about Israel's way of life was built around, and found its meaning in, the blood of the sacrifice at the altar of worship. Without question or challenge, redemption was the theme and the basis for worship in Israel.

Just as redemption was the foundation of worship for Israel, redemption is still the foundation of worship for us. We can only approach God, to seek His forgiveness of our sins, predicated on the blood sacrifice of Christ on Calvary's Cross. We cannot even come before the Lord to offer Him our prayers and our worship, apart from the shed blood of Christ.

Our understanding of the pattern of worship, as set forth in the Tabernacle of Moses, will give meaning and direction to our ministry of worship before the Lord. Each regulation of the law gave insight to as to how God desired their lives to be structured and lived out before Him. Each function of the priesthood in the administration of the offerings, the feasts, and the daily service to the Tabernacle of Moses, carried special revelation of how worship was to be exacted. Their adherence to these regulations assured Israel that their worship would not only be acceptable to the Lord, but pleasing as well.

The pattern of worship, as set forth in the Tabernacle of Moses, was but a shadow of eternal truths that grant us insight and understanding in our approach and presentation of worship. Today, we do not approach God by way of an animal sacrifice; rather, we come before God by way of the sacrifice of Christ, God's Lamb, at Calvary. Today, we do not need a High Priest to represent us before God, as we all have access to God through our High Priest, Jesus Christ; therefore, we do not need the priesthood of men to perform our ministry of prayer, praise, or worship to God. Instead, each of us is a ministering priest who may offer up spiritual sacrifices acceptable to God through Jesus Christ.

We do not need to fret over the keeping of the Law as the basis of our relationship with God, for we have been set free from the letter of the Law. We live by the Law of the Spirit of Christ, through grace. Today, we are not limited to certain days of feasting or religious festivals; wherein, we offer to God the thanksgiving of our hearts in praise.

Every day, from the rising of the sun to the setting of the same, is a day full of the blessings of our God. Our lives are to be continual offerings of living praise that will glorify His Name in the earth. Our understanding of how God led and positioned them to be ministers to Him, will help us as we seek to become effective ministers to God in our ministry of worship.

Natural Israel is a type or a shadow of spiritual Israel, the New Testament Church. God's Word admonishes spiritual Israel, the Church, to learn from the successes and the failures as seen in natural Israel.

> *"Moreover, brethren, I do not want you to be unaware that all our fathers were under the cloud, all passed through the sea, all were baptized into Moses in the cloud and in the*

sea, all ate the same spiritual food, and all drank the same spiritual drink. For they drank of that spiritual Rock that followed them, and that Rock was Christ. But with most of them God was not well pleased, for their bodies were scattered in the wilderness. Now these things became our examples, to the intent that we should not lust after evil things as they also lusted. And do not become idolaters as were some of them. As it is written, 'The people sat down to eat and drink, and rose up to play.' Nor let us commit sexual immorality, as some of them did, and in one day twenty-three thousand fell; nor let us tempt Christ, as some of them also tempted, and were destroyed by serpents; nor complain, as some of them also complained, and were destroyed by the destroyer. Now all these things happened to them as examples, and they were written for our admonition, upon whom the ends of the ages have come" (I Corinthians 10:1-11).

Literally, the Church is to duplicate Israel's successes, and avoid Israel's failures.

Chapter Three

WORSHIP IS ROOTED IN DELIVERANCE

The story of God's deliverance of Israel, from the bondage and oppression of Egypt, is a dramatic one. Israel learned the hard way the cost of failing to adhere to the call of God in their hearts to worship and serve the Lord. The ensuing result of their failure was that they found themselves enslaved in the land of Egypt under the oppressive hand of Pharaoh. Pharaoh continually scoffed at, and challenged, their unseen God; for he desired the worship and service of the people of Israel.

Israel, Abraham's covenant seed of promise, rapidly multiplied and soon grew into a very large nation of people dwelling in the land of Egypt. *"But the children of Israel were fruitful and increased abundantly, multiplied and grew exceedingly mighty; and the land was filled with them"* (Exodus 1:7).

Favor had been granted to the children of Israel because of the positions of honor that had been bestowed on their forefather, Joseph. However, a Pharaoh came to the throne of Egypt who had absolutely no regard for Joseph, or the Israelites. As a matter of fact, he was very fearful of them. He feared that due to their rapid growth, the Israelites might one day turn on the Egyptians and eventually take over the land of Egypt.

Pharaoh's fear soon turned to hate. He decided to remove any favor that the Israelites enjoyed in the land; which resulted in them becoming his slaves. Pharaoh not only wanted to use their labor to increase his kingdom, but through their labor, he sought to break their spirits which would ensure the Egyptian's dominance over the Israelites. The Israelites experienced being dominated in the physical aspect of slavery, as well as, being dominated emotionally, and spiritually.

It is important to understand that it was not the fear and hatred in the heart of Pharaoh that brought the Israelites into the position of slavery. Pharaoh was merely the instrument God used to get Israel's attention; thus, they would be drawn back to His divine purpose for them in the earth. That purpose was the same for Adam as it has been for every man: to worship God and to rule over the works of God's hands.

During the 400 years of dwelling in the land of Egypt, Israel had forsaken their forefather's covenant with the Lord. They turned with fascination to the gods of Egypt, and began to worship them, instead of the God of Abraham, Isaac, and Jacob. They forgot about the God of Joseph who delivered their forefathers from the great famine which had threatened to wipe out the founding families of their nation. As a result of their forsaking the Lord, and their failure to keep their covenant relationship with God, they found themselves in slavery to the Egyptians.

With every passing year, the hardships of the children of Israel grew worse. Bitter, dejected, and full of despair, Israel cried out to God for His mercy and help. They prayed day and night in the feeble hope that God would hear their prayers, and deliver them from the hands of the Egyptians. God heard their prayers and cries for His help; and because of His great love for His people, God set in motion their deliverance from the hand of Pharaoh.

God, in His great mercy, laid the foundation for Israel's redemption from their sin. Redemption was necessary due to their failure to keep the conditions of their covenant relationship. Their redemption would be secured through the sacrifice and the blood of the Passover lamb.

On the backside of the desert, tending his father-in-law's sheep, God had positioned Moses—the vessel He would use to deliver Israel. It was God's plan to use Moses to answer the prayers of His people and deliver them from the bondage of Egypt. God spoke to Moses from the midst of the burning bush and commissioned him to go before the most powerful man in the earth, Pharaoh: He was to demand Israel's freedom from slavery. *"Now therefore, behold, the cry of the children of Israel has come to Me, and I have also seen the oppression with which the Egyptians oppress them. Come now, therefore, and I will send you to Pharaoh that you may bring My people, the children of Israel, out of Egypt"* (Exodus 3:9-10).

As one might imagine, Moses was completely overwhelmed with God's commission to him. He responded with various reasons of why he was not the right man for the assignment. God redirected Moses' focus from his natural inadequacies to the promise of His presence. God's presence would enable Moses to accomplish what He had commissioned Moses to do; deliver His people out of the bondage of Egypt.

God revealed to Moses that the issue of worship was the very center of His purpose in delivering Israel from Egypt. God wanted to deliver Israel from bondage, and to redeem them from their sins, so that He could receive their worship once again. *"So He said, 'I will certainly be with you. And this shall be a sign to you that I have sent you: When you have brought the people out of Egypt, you shall serve God on this mountain'"* (Exodus 3:12).

God instructed Aaron to assist in the commission that had been given to Moses. Moses and Aaron gathered the elders of the people together and informed them of the good news: God had seen their affliction and had heard their prayers. Aaron told the elders that God would deliver them out of the hands of Pharaoh. When the people heard the news, they not only believed Moses and Aaron, but they also bowed down before the Lord and worshiped Him. Worship was the heart of the message that was given to Pharaoh.

Worship became the issue that Pharaoh wrestled with in his decision, of whether or not, to let the Israelites go. Pharaoh believed himself to be a deity that was worthy of worship: he believed that he was the human manifestation of the sun god, Ra.

> *"Afterward Moses and Aaron went in and told Pharaoh, 'Thus says the Lord God of Israel: "Let My people go, that they may hold a feast to Me in the wilderness."' And Pharaoh said, 'Who is the Lord, that I should obey His voice to let Israel go? I do not know the Lord, nor will I let Israel go'"* (Exodus 5:1-2).

If Pharaoh released the Israelites to go into the wilderness and worship their God, he would be admitting that there was a God who was greater and more powerful than himself. Not only was there an economic impact in letting the Israelites go that must be considered, there was the issue of their worship.

God hardened the heart of Pharaoh towards the Israelites; therefore, Pharaoh denied their request. The reason that God hardened his heart was to not only show Israel His great and awesome power, but to show His power to the Egyptians as well. God would prove to all men that He was the only true and living God, and that He alone is worthy of worship. Through His deliverance of Israel, God would gain a great victory over His enemies, and also bring great glory to His name in the earth.

God sent a series of ten plagues on the Egyptians, the last of which cost them the life of the first-born male of every household, including Pharaoh's. Through each of the plagues, God answered Pharaoh's challenge for the rights to His people. It was only after experiencing the devastation and suffering brought about by the death of the first-born male in every home; that Pharaoh conceded to the wishes of God and released the people.

However, the plagues that God sent into the land did not affect the Israelites. Before the last and most devastating plague, God instructed the people as to their responsibility in keeping the final plague—the plague of death—from touching their families. Israel's protection would only be provided through their absolute obedience to the strict observance of the sacrifice of the Passover lamb and the application of its blood to the doorposts.

The sacrifice of the Passover lamb becomes the act of worship that would bring protection to the Israelites. Israel's obedience would not only declare their faith in the Lord, but it would also ensure their deliverance from Pharaoh and the bondage of Egypt. It was a bitter night of sorrows for the Egyptians. However, it was a night of rejoicing for the Israelites; for in the middle of the night, Pharaoh released the Israelites to depart from the land of Egypt.

As Israel was marching out of the land, Pharaoh's heart stirred with anger and revenge. He gathered his army and set out in pursuit of the Israelites. Camped along the shores of the Red Sea, Israel saw the clouds of dust rising from the earth which signaled Pharaoh's rapid approach. The Israelites realized that they were trapped by the Red Sea on one side, and Pharaoh and his army on the other. Not realizing that this final showdown was being orchestrated by God, the Israelites were stricken with fear. Moses entreated the people not to be afraid, but to stand in faith and witness the Lord work on their behalf.

One of the greatest miracles ever witnessed on the earth took place on the shores of the Red Sea. God opened the Red Sea before the Israelites and then commanded them to pass over to the other side. As they moved through the divided sea, Pharaoh and his army entered the passage in the sea. When the Israelites were safe on the other shore, and the armies of Pharaoh were in the midst of the sea, the walls of water that stood obediently open for the Israelites came crashing down on the Egyptians. Without exception, Pharaoh and his army all drowned that day in the sea.

Witnessing this mighty miracle of God, Israel realized that God had indeed delivered them out of the hands of Pharaoh, once and for all. The nation of Israel realized just how foolish they had been in worshiping the inferior and false gods of Egypt. They began to rejoice and sing aloud the praises of God. *"The Lord is my strength and song, and He has become my salvation; He is my God, and I will praise Him; My father's God, and I will exalt Him"* (Exodus 15:2). They sang about the Lord's uniqueness, and the greatness of His power. *"Who is like You, O Lord, among the gods? Who is like You, glorious in holiness, fearful in praises, doing wonders"* (Exodus 15:11)?

Aaron's sister, Miriam, led all the women in a great celebration before the Lord. They sang about His great acts of deliverance, and danced with joy over the victory that the Lord had won.

> *"Then Miriam the prophetess, the sister of Aaron, took the timbrel in her hand; and all the women went out after her with timbrels and with dances. And Miriam answered them: 'Sing to the Lord, for He has triumphed gloriously! The horse and its rider He has thrown into the sea'"* (Exodus 15:20-21)!

Chapter Four

WORSHIP IN THE COVENANT LAW

Israel found they were enslaved in Egypt because of their failure to worship God. The reason God commanded their release from Pharaoh's hand was for the purpose of worship. It was the action of worship, in the sacrifice of the Passover lamb, which gained their deliverance and atonement for their sin. It was the celebration in worship that sealed their deliverance at the Red Sea.

Worship was the reason for Israel's redemption, and redemption was the foundation of Israel's worship. The pattern was created in the heart of God and established in the hearts of His people; worship was to flow out of the hearts of the redeemed.

Israel reached the Wilderness of the Sinai almost three months after their deliverance from the land of Egypt. They set up their camp at the base of Mount Sinai. It was here on Mount Sinai, that God would meet with Moses and reveal His desire to enter into a special covenant of relationship with His people. This covenant is referred to as the Mosaic Covenant, because it was Moses who represented the people before the Lord.

The Mosaic Covenant did not annul, or replace, the Abrahamic Covenant. The covenant that God cut with Abraham was to be eternal, in that, God confirmed all the promises of the covenant with an oath. The Mosaic Covenant was simply added alongside the Abrahamic Covenant because of Israel's sin against God, and their failure to keep the Abrahamic Covenant.

The Mosaic Covenant and the Abrahamic Covenant both flow into, and find their fulfillment in, the Cross of Christ. Without exception, all of their ceremonial elements are both fulfilled, and abolished, in the Cross. Again, without exception, all of their spiritual elements are established and fulfilled in the New Covenant.

The whole of Israel's life was regulated by the Mosaic Covenant. These regulations included their relationships to their families, their relationship to their neighbors, and their relationship to God. All of the promises, as set forth in the Mosaic Covenant, were predicated on Israel's obedience to the conditions of that covenant.

The Mosaic Covenant can be separated into five basic foundational aspects. Our understanding of these will unlock the secrets of worship that they contain as they are relevant and vital to us today. However, within this study, we will concentrate on the first foundational aspect—the Covenant Law.

The first foundational aspect of the Mosaic Covenant was the Covenant Law. The Covenant Law could be broken into three sections. The first section was the "Moral Law." The Moral Law was given in the form of the Ten Commandments, and God gave these commandments to Israel in three forms. First, He spoke them to Moses on Mount Sinai. Secondly, God gave Israel the commandments that He, with His finger, wrote on tablets of stone. Thirdly, God gave the commandments to Israel by writing them on their hearts.

The Ten Commandments were actually a covenant of love between God and Israel, and the covenant contract could only be fulfilled through mutual expressions of love. Israel soon realized that the first five commandments dealt with their relationship to God, and the last five commandments dealt with their relationship to their neighbors.

The Moral Law was not given to Israel to create hardships in their lives but, rather, to bring them into the greatest measure of success and fulfillment in life that was possible. Israel learned the principles that are still true today; that only as they were successful in fulfilling their responsibilities to God, could they successfully fulfill their responsibilities to their neighbor.

The second section of the Covenant Law was the "Civil Law." The Civil Law was an expanded and detailed explanation of the Moral Law. Basically, the Civil Law dealt with, and governed, Israel's responsibilities and codes of conduct with each other. Obedience to the Civil Law required Israel to love the Lord to the degree, that their love for Him influenced their love and conduct towards each other. This is still the pattern for our treatment and consideration of each other today. We must let our deep devotion, and our love for the Lord, be the motivating force that governs our relationships with people.

The third section of the Covenant Law was the "Ceremonial Law." The Ceremonial Law was also an expanded explanation of the Moral Law. The Ceremonial law specifically dealt with Israel's responsibilities to God. Detailed instructions were set forth that regulated the religious administrations of the Tabernacle of Moses: the functions and responsibilities of the priesthood; the observances of the various feasts; and the observance of the various offerings.

Fulfillment of the Ceremonial Law demanded the strictest adherence to each and every regulation. There was no room for any compromise, alteration, or deemed improvements, regardless of how well intentioned they were. Failure to strictly observe the letter of the law would ultimately result in God's rejection of the observance or offering which would remove all spiritual significance and blessing that would have resulted from their obedience.

The Covenant Law teaches us several important truths. Our relationship with God in the New Covenant is based on mutual expressions of love. God still desires holiness from His people, and yet our holiness is not derived from keeping the letter of the law. Through Jesus, we have been set free from the letter of the law so that we might embrace the Spirit of the law in Christ Jesus. The Word sets forth the parameters of grace that governs our walk of holiness before God.

Love, expressed in obedience, is an expression of worship. The Word of the Lord clearly sets forth those expressions of worship that the Father desires from His people. Failure to come before God in worship, according to His desired and prescribed pattern, reduces our worship and activity to mere religious ritual: Religious ritual is void of any significance, power, or blessing.

The Covenant Law foreshadows Jesus Christ for He kept and completely fulfilled the Law, in each and every aspect. He fulfilled the Moral and the Civil Law through His teachings and through His example for living. Jesus was motivated to obedience by His deep love for His Father, and an overwhelming desire to please Him. *"And He who sent Me is with Me. The Father has not left Me alone, for I always do those things that please Him"* (John 8:29).

Jesus abolished the Ceremonial Law through the shedding of

His blood and His death on the Cross. He was the final sacrifice for the sins of mankind. Through His blood, once and for all time, the penalty for man's sin was paid in full, and there will never be another sacrifice needed to cleanse man from his sins.

> *"By that will we have been sanctified through the offering of the body of Jesus Christ once for all. And every priest stands ministering daily and offering repeatedly the same sacrifices, which can never take away sins. But this Man, after He had offered one sacrifice for sins forever, sat down at the right hand of God"* (Hebrews 10:10-12).

The blood of Jesus did for mankind what the continual offerings of blood from sacrificial animals could never do. Through Jesus' blood our sins are forgiven, our conscience is purged, our lives are redeemed from destruction, and we are made members of the family of God.

> *"Not with the blood of goats and calves, but with His own blood He entered the Most Holy Place once for all, having obtained eternal redemption. For if the blood of bulls and goats and the ashes of a heifer, sprinkling the unclean, sanctifies for the purifying of the flesh, how much more shall the blood of Christ, who through the eternal Spirit offered Himself without spot to God, cleanse your conscience from dead works to serve the living God"* (Hebrews 9:12-14)?

Jesus completely fulfilled the Law of God; therefore, all the judgment of the Law has been given to Him. Through His obedience to the Father's will, Jesus has become the only one qualified to be our Judge. *"For the Father judges no one, but has committed all judgment to the Son"* (John 5:22).

The purpose of the Law was to point men to Christ. The Law exposed man's inability to fulfill the Law; thus, his deep need for the grace and mercy of God in his life as found in Galatians 3:24, *"Therefore the law was our tutor to bring us to Christ, that we might be justified by faith."*

Our lives are not redeemed from sin because we keep the Law; neither is it the keeping of the Law that brings us into the family of God. We only have access to the Father through our faith in Jesus Christ, His Son.

> *"But when the fullness of the time had come, God sent forth His Son, born of a woman, born under the law, to redeem those who were under the law, that we might receive the adoption as sons. And because you are sons, God has sent forth the Spirit of His Son into your hearts, crying out, 'Abba, Father!' Therefore you are no longer a slave but a son, and if a son, then an heir of God through Christ"* (Galatians 4:4-7).

Chapter Five

WORSHIP IS THE MINISTRY OF THE PRIESTHOOD

God revealed to Moses on Mount Sinai His desire for Israel to become a kingdom of priests that would faithfully minister before Him. As a kingdom of priests, they would naturally be required to become a holy nation as well. In essence, their lives were to be set apart in holiness from all the other nations and cultures.

Israel was to be completely dedicated to their priestly duties and service before God. God not only wanted Israel to serve Him in a holy priesthood, but He wanted all men everywhere to do the same. Israel was to be the example of worship that would inspire and lead all the other nations of the world in the worship of God.

> *"Now therefore, if you will indeed obey My voice and keep My covenant, then you shall be a special treasure to Me above all people; for all the earth is Mine. And you shall be to Me a kingdom of priests and a holy nation. These are the words which you shall speak to the children of Israel"* (Exodus 19:5-6).

While Moses was on the mountain receiving these instructions, about the priesthood of the Israelites, the children of Israel became impatient and they rebelled against God. They turned their devotion and worship away from the God who had just delivered them from slavery in Egypt, and gave their worship to a calf molded in gold. This violation of their priesthood, before they could even be dedicated to service as priests, so grieved the heart of God, that He rejected their priesthood.

God instituted His priestly order from the tribe of Levi; however, God chose Aaron to be His High Priest through a miraculous sign to the people. It was Aaron's responsibility to be the mediator between God and the people. He was charged with the responsibility of administering the rites of sacrifice, and the presentation of the blood before the Lord, for the atonement of Israel's sins. Aaron was responsible to labor in intercessory prayer on behalf of the people. Literally, Aaron carried the spiritual weight of the entire nation on his shoulders.

We see in Aaron a foreshadowing of Jesus Christ and His ministry as our High Priest. Jesus was our mediator in bringing us into the new covenant relationship with God. *"And for this reason He is the Mediator of the new covenant, by means of death, for the redemption of the transgressions under the first covenant, that those who are called may receive the promise of the eternal inheritance"* (Hebrews 9:15). Jesus, as our High Priest, is seated at the right hand of the Father where He continually offers to God His intercessory prayers on our behalf. *"Therefore He is also able to save to the uttermost those who come to God through Him, since He always lives to make intercession for them"* (Hebrews 7:25).

Jesus, as our High Priest, is very acquainted with the sorrows and trials that we face in this life. He cares deeply about our heartaches and is, in fact, touched by that which touches us. What happens to us matters to Him, for He feels what we are experiencing and he feels what we are feeling. Jesus invites us to come boldly before Him and seek His help and mercy in our lives for He understands and cares about our needs.

> *"For we have not an High Priest which cannot be touched with the feeling of our infirmities; but was in all points tempted like as we are, yet without sin. Let us therefore come boldly unto the throne of grace that we may obtain mercy, and find grace to help in time of need"* (Hebrews 4:15-16).

As earlier stated, all of the priests in Israel were from the tribe of Levi; however, not all of the Levites were priests. Only the sons of Aaron, and their subsequent family lineage, were to serve as priests. This points out to us today, that only through Jesus, can we become members of God's family; thus, fulfilling our priesthood.

There were basically three areas of service that the priests were to perform. Their first and foremost responsibility was to minister before the Lord with their prayers and their offerings of incense in worship. Secondly, they were responsible to serve before the Brazen

Altar. It was at the Brazen Altar that sacrifices were offered, not only to please the Lord, but to meet the needs of the people in atoning for their sins. And thirdly, their responsibility was to minister to the people as they taught them to obey the laws of God and to follow in His ways.

Today, God has called and assigned each and every believer to become a priest before Him.

> *"And they sang a new song, saying: 'You are worthy to take the scroll, and to open its seals; For You were slain, and have redeemed us to God by Your blood out of every tribe and tongue and people and nation, and have made us kings and priests to our God; and we shall reign on the earth'"* (Revelation 5:9-10).

It is our responsibility as priests, to continually offer to the Lord our sacrifices of praise, and the worship of our hearts. We are instructed in the Word of the Lord that the fruit of our lips is to be praise, and the response of our hearts is to be worship. *"You also, as living stones, are being built up a spiritual house, a holy priesthood, to offer up spiritual sacrifices acceptable to God through Jesus Christ"* (I Peter 2:5).

As with Adam, God intends for there to be two powerful streams flowing from the life of every believer. The first stream is to be our worship of God. The second stream is to be that of exercising dominion over the works of God's hands in the earth. Our worship and our ruler-ship are tied together and actually flow out of each other. The effectiveness of our ruler-ship, in reigning victoriously over the various areas of our life, is proportionately tied to the depth and sincerity of our worship.

God has called us to be a royal priesthood, or in other words, a ruling priesthood. This priesthood will enable us to live above our circumstances, instead of our circumstances ruling over us. We may not be able to change or alter our circumstances, but we can guard our hearts and realize, that through the offering of our praise, we position ourselves for the Lord to work. We can then be assured that what has been meant for our harm and destruction, the Lord will turn around for our good.

We generally have the same three areas of responsibilities in ministry that were assigned to the Aaronic priesthood. First, and foremost, we are to minister to the Lord in our offerings of praise and worship. Secondly, we are responsible to minister to one another in our prayers of intercession; we are to bear one another's burdens; and we are to encourage one another in the Word. Thirdly, we, as priests, are to minister to those outside of Christ; as we are a witness to them of God's love and power.

Our priesthood is to be characterized by holiness. Our holiness is not just relegated to our outer man, but it is actually to be evidenced in our character as well. As priests to the Lord, we are to be separated from the world and separated to the service of our God.

Just as with Israel, our praise and worship is to be the outflow of Christ's work of redemption in our lives. The priests of the Old Covenant could not approach God apart from the presentation of the sacrificial blood. Even so, we cannot approach God apart from the shed blood of Jesus. The blood of Jesus applied in our lives, releases us to fulfill our ministries as priests before the Lord.

There were several offerings that were presented to the Lord as a part of Israel's worship. The strict regulations found in each of the offerings brought significance and meaning to Israel's worship.

The most precious offering out of all the offerings, in the eyes of the Lord, was "THE BURNT OFFERING." This offering, placed on the altar, was to be wholly burnt or consumed. There was not to be any part of this offering divided out to the priests, which was customary in other offerings; the offering in its entirety, belonged to the Lord.

The Burnt Offering, being wholly consumed in the fires of the altar, signified the complete dedication of the worshiper to God, and that the worshiper was withholding nothing from the Lord. The worship that the Lord received from the worshiper was precious because it was given voluntarily from the heart. This offering demonstrated the worshiper's total abandonment, and obedience, to the will of the Lord. The aroma from the offering, as it ascended from the altar, was a sweet savor to the Lord.

There were various grades of offerings that were presented on the altar before the Lord; an ox or a bullock, a sheep or a goat, a turtle dove or a pigeon might have been selected as the appropriate offering. Depending on the need, each offering often denoted the worshiper's level of understanding concerning the requirements of the Lord, or his position in life—or most often, his depth of commitment to the Lord. Yet, when presented before the Lord as an offering from the heart, it was accepted.

Today, there are various levels of understanding and commitment to the Lord within the Body of Christ. Worship that is offered from a dedicated and willful heart is accepted by the Lord, regardless of the level of understanding. Worship from the altar of our heart ascends to the Lord as a sweet-smelling savor and is considered precious to the heart of the Lord.

The Burnt Offering points us to Jesus and His total abandonment to the will of His Father. He offered Himself voluntarily on the altar of the Cross to be consumed as the payment for the sins of mankind.

> *"Sacrifice and offering You did not desire; My ears You have opened. Burnt offering and sin offering You did not require. Then I said, 'Behold, I come; In the scroll of the book it is written of me. I delight to do Your will, O my God, and Your law is within my heart'"* (Psalms 40:6-8).

"THE MEAL OFFERING" was always offered in conjunction with the Burnt Offering. It was the only bloodless offering offered on the altar. This offering was voluntary and testified to the fact that the worshiper owed everything to the Lord. With a heart full of gratitude and thanksgiving for the abundant blessings of God, the worshiper presented his offering on the altar. The Meal Offering consisted of fine flour, oil, and frankincense. The priests would divide among themselves a certain portion of this offering, and then the remaining portion was placed before the Lord on the altar to be burned.

The Meal Offering speaks to us about the attitude of our hearts as we enter into worship before the Lord. We are to be grateful for the abundant blessings of the Lord in our lives. The presentation of the Meal Offering was not to be just the formality of a ritual; rather, the worshiper was to come before the Lord with his offering and enjoy the fellowship of the Lord.

Worship is not to be viewed as an obligation, which is based on a performance that will appease the heart of God for a season. Instead, our worship should be a meaningful time of fellowship in which we feed on the richness and blessing of His presence. Our worship of the Lord should never be presented through a sense of duty; rather, our worship should always proceed out of a heart full of desire and gratitude to the Lord.

The Meal Offering points out the person, nature, and character of Jesus. The fine flour speaks to us of Christ's sinless humanity. Today, as believers, we share in Christ's victory over sin; for Jesus has delivered us from the power of sin and He declares that sin shall not have dominion over our lives.

The oil represents to us the anointing of the Holy Spirit that rested on Christ. Every miracle Jesus worked in the lives of people in need, was by the anointing and the power of the Holy Spirit. Available to every believer is the same anointing and power of the Holy Spirit to accomplish the work of ministry; thereby, fulfilling our priesthood. We can walk every day of our lives filled with the anointing and the power of the precious Spirit of God.

The frankincense characterizes the different graces of the Holy Spirit that were evident in the life of Christ. Through the representation of the frankincense we can see the fruit of the Holy Spirit produced in the life of the believer, when the heart of the believer is fully surrendered to the Lord.

The next offering to be considered was called "THE PEACE OFFERING." The Peace Offering involved the sacrifice of a selected and qualified animal. The worshiper was to lay his hands on the head of the animal and confess his sins and transgressions. Then the worshiper was to personally kill the sacrifice; thereby, through the death of the sacrifice, the worshiper gained peace with God.

The fat was to be separated from the animal and placed on the altar where it would be consumed. After the fat was removed, and presented before the Lord on the altar, the remaining portions of the offering were divided between the priest and the worshiper. At this point everyone, among whom the sacrifice was divided, ate and fellowshipped together.

The Peace Offering was a voluntary offering to the Lord to show the gratitude of the worshiper for the Lord's kindness and blessings. The Peace Offering also points us to Christ, whose sacrificial death on the Cross brought us peace with God. We are reminded to come before the Lord with our worship and feast on the kindness of God; whereby, He grants us His perfect peace. *"And by Him to reconcile all things to Himself, by Him, whether things on earth or things in heaven, having made peace through the blood of His cross"* (Colossians 1:20).

The first three offerings, we have discussed, were all free-will offerings. The remaining offerings were not voluntary, but rather mandatory to all of Israel. The first of these two compulsory offerings was, "THE SIN OFFERING." The Sin Offering involved the death of the sacrificial animal with regard to specific sins and transgressions of the worshiper. Only through the shedding of blood could their sins be forgiven and cleansed. The priest would take the blood of the sacrifice, and present it before the Lord, so that the sins of the worshiper could be forgiven.

The Sin Offering dealt with the specific sins that had been committed, as well as, dealing with the very sinful nature of the worshiper; therefore, a sacrifice must be offered for each sin committed. However, dealing with specific sins, without addressing the fallen nature of man, was simply futile and endless. The nature of man does not fully comprehend the ways of the Lord, largely due to the nature of man, which is at war with God.

The Sin Offering points us to the sacrifice on the Cross. Through His shed blood, our sins are forgiven and forever cleansed. Through His death, Jesus dealt with our sinful and rebellious natures that were at war with God.

> *"But now in Christ Jesus you who once were far off have been brought near by the blood of Christ. For He Himself is our peace, who has made both one, and has broken down the middle wall of separation, having abolished in His flesh the enmity, that is, the law of commandments contained in*

> *ordinances, so as to create in Himself one new man from the two, thus making peace, and that He might reconcile them both to God in one body through the cross, thereby putting to death the enmity"* (Ephesians 2:13-16).

The last offering to consider is the "THE TRESPASS OFFERING." The Trespass Offering was very closely related to the Sin Offering and it is very difficult to draw much of a distinction between the two. Both offerings were compulsory to the worshiper, and often were presented before the Lord at the same time. The similarities of the Trespass Offering and the Sin Offering involve the offense of sin. In both cases, however, the sins that are committed, are committed against God, and must be atoned for by the shedding of blood.

The Sin Offering deals with sin that is committed against God, and has a negative affect on the sinner. The Trespass Offering also involves sin that is committed against God; however, it involves a sin committed against, or involving another person. While all sin is against God, not all sin involves another person. The offender was required to present a sacrifice before the Lord to atone for his sin. He was also required to make restitution to the offended parties.

The Trespass Offering points us to Jesus, who paid our sacrifice for sin on the Cross. Jesus paid for all of our sins—those that were committed against God, as well as, those committed against our fellow man. The Word of the Lord teaches us that we are to seek the forgiveness of those whom we have wronged or offended and, where possible, make restitution. We are to forgive those who have wronged or offended us, based on the fact that God has forgiven us such a tremendous debt.

> *"And whenever you stand praying, if you have anything against anyone, forgive him that your Father in heaven may also forgive you your trespasses. But if you do not forgive, neither will your Father in heaven forgive your trespasses"* (Mark 11:25-26).

Out of all the feasts of Israel, there were three feasts that the

Lord required Israel to observe. Represented in these feasts are truths that will enhance our understanding of today's worship.

The first feast we will consider is "THE FEAST OF PASSOVER." The Feast of Passover is the celebration of God's divine deliverance of Israel from the bondage of Egypt. Just as on the night of their exodus from Egypt, this feast required the sacrifice of a lamb without spot or blemish. This feast served as a yearly reminder to Israel of their deliverance through the blood of the lamb on the doorposts. They remembered and, therefore, celebrated the fact that through the application of the blood, the judgment of God passed over their family and they were delivered from Pharaoh's oppressive hand.

Just as Israel was spared the judgment of God through the blood of the lamb, even so today, we are spared God's judgment through the blood of God's Lamb, Jesus Christ. *"But God demonstrates His own love toward us, in that while we were still sinners, Christ died for us. Much more then, having now been justified by His blood, we shall be saved from wrath through Him"* (Romans 5:8-9).

In the celebration of the Passover we see Jesus, as God's Lamb, sacrificed on the altar of the Cross. The blood of Jesus, God's Lamb, is to be applied to the doorposts of our hearts if we are to escape God's judgment of our sins. Only through the blood of Jesus can we be cleansed of our sins and delivered from the power of sin.

Each and every day we must come before the Lord, in the celebration of worship, and freely express the gratitude of our hearts for being delivered from the bondage of sin. *"But you are a chosen generation, a royal priesthood, a holy nation, His own special people, that you may proclaim the praises of Him who called you out of darkness into His marvelous light"* (I Peter 2:9).

The second feast to consider is "THE FEAST OF PENTECOST." The Feast of Pentecost took place fifty days after the Feast of the Passover. The Feast of Pentecost is the celebration of the first-fruits of the wheat harvest. They celebrated the Lord's kindness and faithful provision in their lives, through the abundance of the harvest.

The Feast of Pentecost was also a celebration of the giving of the Tablets of Law that were given to Moses on Mount Sinai. Israel celebrated the giving of the Law, for through the Law, structure was given to their daily lives. Actually, the Law taught Israel how to live before the Lord.

The Feast of Pentecost points us to Christ and His resurrection from the dead. Jesus became the first-fruits from the dead when He broke the bonds of death. Through His victory over death, we also can share in Christ's resurrection.

> *"But now Christ is risen from the dead, and has become the first-fruits of those who have fallen asleep. For since by man came death, by Man also came the resurrection of the dead. For as in Adam all die, even so in Christ all shall be made alive"* (I Corinthians 15:20-22).

The Feast of Pentecost also points us to the ministry of the Holy Spirit. On the day of Pentecost, exactly fifty days after Passover, God poured out the gift of the Holy Spirit on the 120 believers that were present. So profound was this outpouring that 3,000 people were saved, and they became the first-fruits of the spiritual resurrection and harvest.

Today, it is vitally important that we do not take our gift of eternal life for granted. Jesus paid a very high price for our salvation; whereby, we are delivered from sin and redeemed from death. We must never fail to offer God our praise and worship for delivering us from the bonds of death. Through Christ's victory over death, even the fear of death has been removed.

We need to offer praise to God for giving us His Word; for by His Word, we can structure our lives. Building our life on the Word of the Lord will ensure our stability in hard times and our ultimate victory over the devil. The privilege of walking in the fullness and the power of the Holy Spirit, on a daily basis, invokes a deep response of praise and worship in our hearts to the Lord.

The last feast we will consider is "THE FEAST OF TABERNACLES." The Feast of Tabernacles is the festive celebration of God's provision and guidance in the wilderness journey and it took place at the end of the fruit harvest. All of the Israelites would dwell in booths for a period of seven days in order to help them remember the days of dwelling in tents during the wilderness journey. During these seven days they would celebrate, as they remembered the faithfulness of God in His daily provisions for them.

The dwelling in booths also served as a reminder to Israel, that the tents in which they dwelt in the wilderness, were not their final home. God had promised them a land flowing with milk and honey, and by faith, they believed God would keep His word to them. Therefore, they set their hopes and affections on that land of promise. Their worship of God in this feast expressed their faith in God; knowing He would continue to provide for them until He established them in the land of promise.

The Feast of Tabernacles is a reminder to us that we are not citizens of this world; rather, we are citizens of Heaven. Our life on earth is only preparation for our eternal home in our land of promise—Heaven.

> *"These all died in faith, not having received the promises, but having seen them afar off were assured of them, embraced them and confessed that they were strangers and pilgrims on the earth. For those who say such things declare plainly that they seek a homeland. And truly if they had called to mind that country from which they had come out, they would have had opportunity to return. But now they desire a better, that is, a heavenly country. Therefore God is not ashamed to be called their God, for He has prepared a city for them"* (Hebrews 11:13-16).

We are reminded to set our affection on things that are in heaven, and not become bound to our affection of things on earth. That on which we set our affection, becomes that to which we are bound. That on which we set our affection, will dominate our thoughts, our time, our talents, and our energies. *"If then you were raised with Christ, seek those things which are above, where Christ is, sitting at the right hand of God. Set your mind on things above, not on things on the earth"* (Colossians 3:1-2).

By faith, we believe that God will keep His Word to us and will one day take us to dwell in that glorious land of promise; to a city prepared for us—Heaven, our eternal home. Therefore, we lift our hearts in worship to celebrate God's faithfulness to provide for us here on earth; resting in the fact that He will guide us to our land of promise. There, on Heaven's shore, we will dwell in the light of His promise for ever and ever.

> *"Let not your heart be troubled; you believe in God, believe also in Me. In My Father's house are many mansions; if it were not so, I would have told you. I go to prepare a place for you. And if I go and prepare a place for you, I will come again and receive you to Myself; that where I am, there you may be also"* (John 14:1-3).

Chapter Six

WORSHIP PATTERNS IN THE TABERNACLE OF MOSES

The divine purpose for building the Tabernacle of Moses was to provide a place for God to dwell among His redeemed people. Until this time, God had not dwelt with His people since the days of Adam (prior to Adam's rebellion and subsequent fall). God's desire to be close and spend time with His people was very great, so He purposed the Tabernacle of Moses, *"And let them make me a sanctuary; that I may dwell among them"* (Exodus 25:8).

There were several requirements and restrictions placed on Moses in the construction of the Tabernacle. Each of these requirements and restrictions carry important truths that will enhance our worship of the Lord. Though the tabernacle we are constructing today is spiritual, and not of a physical nature, the requirements and the restrictions have not changed.

The Tabernacle was to be built with the free-will offerings of the people. The Israelites were given great riches by the Egyptians on their deliverance from Egypt. This sudden blessing of wealth was not simply to make the Israelites rich; rather, it was to provide the necessary materials that would be needed to construct the Tabernacle. God expected the people to freely give of the blessings that He had provided, so that His plan for the Tabernacle could be fulfilled. Israel's giving was considered by God an expression of worship. Israel realized that God was their source of supply, and they obediently released from that supply, in their worship of God. *"Speak to the children of Israel, that they bring Me an offering. From everyone who gives it willingly with his heart you shall take My offering"* (Exodus 25:2).

Today, we understand that giving is a vital part of worship. We must realize that all of the blessings we enjoy are from the hand of the Lord. These blessings are not in our lives so that we can consume them on our lusts and desires; instead, we are compelled in the Word to release what God has given us, so that the work of the ministry can be accomplished.

The second requirement was that the Tabernacle was to be built by a people whose hearts had been stirred by God. God expected the people to be passionate about the building of His Tabernacle: Indifference and apathy were to have no place in the work of the Lord. *"Then everyone came whose heart was stirred, and everyone whose spirit was willing, and they brought the Lord's offering for the work of the tabernacle of meeting, for all its service, and for the holy garments"* (Exodus 35:21).

Today, we are building the spiritual house of the Lord. We are to be equally as passionate about the work of the Lord as Israel was about the Tabernacle's construction. Just as God would not accept apathy and indifference from Israel, so He will not accept it today in our service before Him.

The third requirement placed on the people was that they must be willing to serve the Lord. God did not want anyone to be forced to serve Him, only those whose hearts were willing. As with God's decision to create mankind, He wanted to be loved and served out of desire, and not out of duty or a sense of obligation.

Today, the Lord still wants His people to come before Him in worship and in service to His name. He wants us to come out a sense of desire, not duty, or obligation. *"Take from among you an offering to the Lord, whoever is of a willing heart and let him bring it as an offering to the Lord: gold, silver, and bronze"* (Exodus 35:5).

The fourth requirement placed on the people was that they were to use the wisdom of God in constructing the Tabernacle and not their own wisdom. God wanted Israel to look to Him as their sole source of wisdom and knowledge. They were not to rely on the wisdom and knowledge of construction that they had acquired in Egypt. *"Then Moses called Bezalel and Aholiab, and every gifted artisan in whose heart the Lord had put wisdom, everyone whose heart was stirred, to come and do the work"* (Exodus 36:2).

Today, we also are to look to the Lord as our sole source of wisdom and knowledge in doing the work of the ministry. We are not to rely on the wisdom and knowledge of the world in order to function in ministry. The wisdom of God is foolishness to the world, but it is righteousness to the believer. God's wisdom is absolutely essential to our success.

The fifth requirement that the Lord placed on the people was that they were to be guided and empowered by the Holy Spirit. The craftsmen and the skilled workers were all gifted by the Holy Spirit and it was this gifting of the Holy Spirit that made their talent effective in the work. *"He has filled him with the Spirit of God, in wisdom and understanding, in knowledge and all manner of workmanship"* (Exodus 35:31).

Today, the Church is totally dependent on the Holy Spirit to gift and empower the believer to do the work of the ministry. Apart from the participation of the Holy Spirit, the work of ministry would be reduced to empty religious ritual; ritual that has a form of godliness, but in reality, is void of God's power.

The last requirement placed on the people was that they were to follow the divine pattern as it was shown to Moses. God commanded Moses to follow every detail He showed him in the construction of the Tabernacle. Moses was not to allow any improvements, alterations, or changes, to be made. The Tabernacle was the most perfect building ever constructed on the earth. It never needed improving, upgrading, or repair, for God's design was perfect. *"And see to it that you make them according to the pattern which was shown you on the mountain"* (Exodus 25:40).

Today, God's divine pattern for our lives and ministries is clearly set forth in His Word. We are not to alter, or try to improve on, God's prescribed plan for living and ministry. In following the ways of the Lord as set forth in His Word, we will see that they are not only right, but His ways are perfect.

A brief mention of the various materials that were used in constructing the Tabernacle would be helpful in our study of redemption. We will not go into depth on any item or color that was used; however, we will mention the spiritual significance of each item. Moses did not have any latitude in choosing the materials that would be used to build the Tabernacle. God, Himself, prescribed even the colors that were to be woven into the fabrics.

We begin with "GOLD" as the gold represents to us the Deity of Christ; and His divine kingly nature, and character. "SILVER" was used to pay the redemption tax that was required of Israel; and silver speaks to us of our redemption through Christ's sacrifice on the Cross. "BRASS" speaks to us about the judgment of God on our sins; for Jesus suffered the judgment of our sins once, and for all.

"PRECIOUS STONES" were used to adorn the High Priest's garments, for they speak to us about Jesus, our High Priest. "FINE LINEN" speaks to us of Christ's purity and His righteousness, and it forever reminds us, that through Jesus, we have been made the righteousness of God. "SHITTIM WOOD" speaks to us of Christ's incorruptible humanity. Jesus was tempted in all points, just like we are, yet He did not yield to sin.

"OIL" speaks to us of the Holy Spirit, and His ministry of lifting up men and pointing them to Jesus. "SPICES FOR THE ANOINTING OIL" speaks to us about the anointing of the Holy Spirit for the work of the ministry. The spices speak to us about the special graces, gifts, and fruit of the Holy Spirit that are to be evident in the believer's life. "SPICES FOR THE SWEET INCENSE" speaks to us about the prayer ministry of Jesus. The variety of spices speaks to us about the various forms of prayer; intercession, petition, praise, worship, and warfare…just to mention a few.

The color "BLUE" speaks to us about the heavenly nature of Christ for He is the Lord of heaven. The color "PURPLE" speaks to us about Christ's royalty and kingship. The color "SCARLET" speaks to us of Christ's blood and sacrifice for our sins.

"GOATS'-HAIR" speaks to us of Christ's taking our sins on Himself, and actually becoming sin, so that we could become God's righteousness. "RAMS' SKIN DYED RED" speaks to us of Christ, Who was our substitute in death and the payment for our sins. "BADGERS'-SKINS" were used as the outermost layer of covering for the Tabernacle. The badgers'-skins speak to us about the covering of Christ over our lives, and His protection from the work of the enemy.

Each of these materials and colors, that have been mentioned, had a specific place, and a specific function, in the ministry of the Tabernacle of Moses. Further study of these materials and colors would prove enriching to the reader.

Worship was at the center of Israel's daily activity. God desired to dwell with His people, and fellowship with them, on a daily basis. The Tabernacle was positioned in the very center of the camp. Every day, this center position in the camp reminded the Israelites that worship and fellowship with God was to be at the very center and core of their daily lives.

To the unbeliever, viewing the Tabernacle from outside the camp, there would be nothing of beauty that would draw them into the Tabernacle. The beauty of the Tabernacle was to be seen and appreciated only from the inside. To the unbeliever, there is nothing in the outward appearance of the Lord or His Church that would, in and of itself, draw them in. *"For He shall grow up before Him as a tender plant, and as a root out of dry ground. He has no form or comeliness; and when we see Him, there is no beauty that we should desire Him"* (Isaiah 53:2). Only as we become a believer, can we truly see and appreciate the overwhelming beauty of Christ; this is also true of worship.

There is nothing in the worship of God that would draw an unbeliever to embrace or even participate in worship. The reason for this is profound; wherein, worship flows out of redemption, and it will never be accepted, or understood, by those who have never been redeemed. The believer must never try to compromise his expressions of worship in an attempt to accommodate, or make his worship palatable to the unbeliever. The only concern of the worshiper should be that God is pleased and is receiving his worship as offered.

Let's take a journey together into the Tabernacle of Moses. The first thing we would notice is the "COURTYARD FENCE." The fence stands seven feet tall and is made of linen that is attached to brass pillars. The white linen represents the righteousness of Christ. The fence that surrounds the Tabernacle area, known as the "OUTER COURT," acted as a barrier between man and God. The fence ensured that there would not be a wrongful approach into God's presence; a wrongful approach that would be brought about by man's sinful nature and condition. The "BRASS PILLARS" speaks to us of God's judgment of sin; however, just as the white linen of the fence covered the brass poles, so the righteousness of Christ covers the believer against the judgment of God.

There is only one "GATE" of entrance into the courtyard, even though the courtyard was open. Unless you came through this one gate, you were not given access into the presence of the Lord. Regardless of your rank or station in life, or whether you were rich or poor, all had to come through the same gate. Jesus is the one and only gate into the family of God, and He is also the only gate into the presence of God. In order to fulfill our destiny of worship and ruler-ship, we must first come into God's presence through Jesus. *"Jesus said to him, 'I am the way, the truth, and the life. No one comes to the Father except through Me'"* (John 14:6).

The first article of furniture encountered when entering through the courtyard gate was "THE BRAZEN ALTAR." The Brazen Altar was a place of death. It was here, at the altar, that the priests would offer the animals in sacrifice for the atonement for sin. Each animal was tied to the horns of the altar, as they were not willing sacrifices. After killing the sacrifice, the blood of the sacrifice was poured out at the base of the altar and the flesh was consumed on the altar. The Brazen Altar was positioned by the gate, and no one could enter the courtyard without first passing the Brazen Altar.

The Brazen Altar represents the altar of Calvary, where Jesus, God's Lamb, was slain. Jesus was a willing sacrifice and was bound to the Cross by His love for us. Today, the only way we can approach God the Father, is through the Cross of Jesus. The Cross forever stands as a reminder to us of the great price Jesus paid for our sins in order to purchase our redemption. It is the blood of Jesus that cleanses us from our sins; thereby we have access to the Father in our worship. *"Knowing that you were not redeemed with corruptible things, like silver or gold, from your aimless conduct received by tradition from your fathers, but with the precious blood of Christ, as of a lamb without blemish and without spot"* (I Peter 1:18-19).

The second article of furniture that we encounter, as we move past the Brazen Altar, is "THE BRAZEN LAVER." The Brazen Laver was positioned between the Brazen Altar, and the tent of the congregation; which was also called the Holy Place. The Brazen Laver was a basin that held water. The chief function and purpose of the laver was for the cleansing of the priests. The priests were not allowed to go into the Holy Place to minister before the Lord with the stains of blood that had been acquired from their ministry at the Brazen Altar.

The bottom of the laver was lined with the looking glasses or the brass mirrors that had been given by the women. The purpose of the mirror was to reflect back the image that was in front of the mirror. The priests would come to the laver to look and see the areas of their person that needed to be cleansed. After washing away the stains of blood, the priest could then progress into the Holy Place and assume their various ministries before the Lord.

The Brazen Laver represents to us the ministry of the Word in our lives. When we look into the Word, we are able to see the areas that do not conform to the standards that are set forth. We become convicted by what we see and, through the Word, we are cleansed. *"That He might sanctify and cleanse her with the washing of water by the Word, that He might present her to Himself a glorious church, not having spot or wrinkle or any such thing, but that she should be holy and without blemish"* (Ephesians 5:26-27). Worship from an impure heart is not acceptable to God. The cleansing power of the Word releases us to worship God from a pure heart.

Moving past the Brazen Laver, we enter into the "HOLY PLACE" and we are confronted with a beauty that is indescribable. The walls of the Holy Place stand fifteen feet tall and are made of gold that is set in silver sockets. Looking up, we see a white linen ceiling that has various colors, and threads of gold woven into its borders.

There are three pieces of furniture in the Holy Place: the Table of Shewbread, the Golden Candlestick, and the Golden Altar of Incense. "THE TABLE OF SHEWBREAD" is positioned on the north wall of the Holy Place, directly opposite of the Golden Candlestick. It is a small table, three feet long, one and one-half feet wide, and two and one-fourth feet tall. The table is made of wood that is overlaid with gold.

Placed on The Table of Shewbread are twelve loaves of bread that have been sprinkled with frankincense. These loaves of bread on the table are presented before the Lord for a period of seven days.

On the Sabbath, the loaves were changed and the old bread was eaten by the priests. The table became the place of fellowship for the priests, and the priests would minister to one another in the breaking of bread together.

The table and the bread both represent Jesus as the Bread of Life, and our Sustainer in life. Jesus said, *"I am the bread of life: he that cometh to Me shall never hunger; and he that believeth on Me shall never thirst"* (John 6:35). Just as the table was the center, and the basis, for the fellowship of the priests, so Jesus is to be the center, and the basis, for our fellowship as believers. Our worship should be centered on Jesus as the only source for our spiritual nourishment. The bread also represents Jesus as the Living Word of God as found in John 6:51, *"I am the living bread which came down from heaven. If anyone eats of this bread, he will live forever; and the bread that I shall give is My flesh, which I shall give for the life of the world."*

Our ministry to one another is to be based on our fellowship in the Word of the Lord. Just as the bread on the table was the only provision for food for the priests, so Jesus is our Bread of Life and is our only provision for spiritual nourishment. He, alone, is our full and satisfying portion in this life, as He is our joy in communion and in fellowship. Jesus is the healer and the source of our health. He, alone, is the full provision for our every need in life. As we fellowship in His Word, we find total fulfillment in His presence. Fulfilled in His presence, our hearts leap with joy, and praise breaks forth from our hearts to Him; for He is our everlasting portion.

"THE GOLDEN CANDLESTICK" was positioned on the south wall of the Holy Place, directly opposite the Table of Shewbread. The Candlestick was made of gold and had seven oil lamps on it. The Golden Candlestick was the only source of light inside the Holy Place, for there were no windows to let in the natural light from the outside. The light from the Golden Candlestick was necessary for the priests to function in their respective ministries inside the Tabernacle. The Golden Candlestick points us to Jesus, Who is the light of the world, *"As long as I am in the world, I am the light of the world"* (John 9:5).

"THE OIL" points us to the Holy Spirit, who anointed Jesus for ministry at His baptism. The priests were to fellowship around the Table of Shewbread, and offer their incense and prayers to God at the Golden Altar of Incense. These two priestly functions were to be done in the light of the Golden Candlestick.

This is a picture of the church and of the believer today. We are to daily walk in the light of His presence and not walk according to the wisdom of this world. We are to perform our ministry as priests under the anointing of the Holy Spirit. Just as the priests daily replenished the oil in the lamps, we are to daily be filled with the Holy Spirit. We are to be the reflection of the light of Jesus. This reflection will shine from our hearts because of the continual supply of the Holy Spirit's anointing.

> *"You are the light of the world. A city that is set on a hill cannot be hidden. Nor do they light a lamp and put it under a basket, but on a lampstand, and it gives light to all who are in the house. Let your light so shine before men, that they may see your good works and glorify your Father in heaven"* (Matthew 5:14-16).

"THE GOLDEN ALTAR OF INCENSE" was positioned directly in front of the Veil that separated the Holy Place from the Holy of Holies. The altar was made of wood that was overlaid with gold; and the purpose of this altar was for the burning of incense before the Lord. The priest would place the incense on the altar to be consumed in its fire. The priest would then offer prayers of intercession on the people's behalf as the smoke, from the burning incense, ascended to the Lord.

The Golden Altar of Incense points us to the ministry of Jesus Christ as our Great High Priest.

> *"Seeing then that we have a great High Priest who has passed through the heavens, Jesus the Son of God, let us hold fast our confession. For we do not have a High Priest who cannot sympathize with our weaknesses, but was in all points tempted as we are, yet without sin"* (Hebrews 4:14-15).

Jesus is seated at the right hand of the Father and daily intercedes on our behalf. *"But He, because He continues forever, has an unchangeable priesthood. Therefore He is also able to save to the uttermost those who come to God through Him, since He always lives to make intercession for them"* (Hebrews 7:24-25).

We also see the ministry of the Holy Spirit at this altar. The Holy Spirit makes intercession for us according to the will of the Lord. Here, at the Golden Altar of Incense, we see the ministry of prayer assigned to every believer. We are to offer the sweet incense of our prayers to the Lord from the altar of our heart. Our prayers then ascend to the Heavenly Sanctuary, before the Throne of God, through the Holy Spirit. There, at the Throne of God, our prayers blend with the intercessory prayers of Jesus Christ, our Great High Priest. The power of God is released when our prayers are offered in worship.

"THE VEIL" was positioned as the dividing partition that separated the Holy Place from the Holy of Holies. The word "veil" actually means, "a separation curtain" or "that which hides." The purpose of the veil was two-fold: first, it was to hide the Shekinah Glory of the Lord from men's eyes; and secondly, it was to keep sinful man separated from the Most Holy God. Only the High Priest was allowed, once a year, to enter behind the Veil and to present the blood of the sacrifice on the Mercy Seat of the Ark of the Covenant.

The Veil points us to Jesus, as He is the dividing partition between sinful man and a Holy God. When Jesus died on the Cross, the Veil in the temple was rent from top to bottom signifying that the way had been opened for all men to come to God. No longer would man need a priest to represent him. Now, through the blood of Jesus, all men may come by faith to the Father.

> *"Therefore, brethren, having boldness to enter the Holiest by the blood of Jesus, by a new and living way which He consecrated for us, through the veil, that is, His flesh, and having a High Priest over the house of God, let us draw near with a true heart in full assurance of faith, having our hearts sprinkled from an evil conscience and our bodies washed with pure water. Let us hold fast the confession of*

our hope without wavering, for He who promised is faithful" (Hebrews 10:19-22).

The final piece of furniture in the Tabernacle of Moses was "THE ARK OF THE COVENANT." The Ark of the Covenant was the most important piece of furniture in many ways, for it actually occupied three different sanctuaries: The Tabernacle of Moses; The Tabernacle of David; and The Temple of Solomon. The Ark was made of wood that was overlaid with gold. Inside the Ark was Aaron's rod that budded, the golden pot of manna, and the broken tablets of the law.

The lid of the Ark was called "THE MERCY SEAT." Once a year, the High Priest would enter the Holy of Holies to present the blood of the sacrifice on the Mercy Seat for the atonement of the peoples' sins. It was here, over the blood-stained Mercy Seat, that God would manifest His presence in His Shekinah cloud of glory for all the people to behold. There was no need for a light source in the Holy of Holies, for it was perpetually lit with the light of His glory.

The Ark speaks to us of Christ's ministry as our great High Priest. After His death on the Cross and His victorious resurrection, Jesus ascended into heaven to enter the Holy of Holies in the Heavenly Tabernacle. There, in the Holy of Holies, Jesus presented His blood on the Mercy Seat before God as payment for man's transgression of God's Law.

> *"But Christ came as High Priest of the good things to come, with the greater and more perfect tabernacle not made with hands, that is, not of this creation. Not with the blood of goats and calves, but with His own blood He entered the Most Holy Place once for all, having obtained eternal redemption"* (Hebrews 9:11-12).

Having obtained our salvation and our redemption, Jesus sat down at the right hand of the Father's throne. *"And every priest stands ministering daily and offering repeatedly the same sacrifices, which can never take away sins. But this Man, after He had offered one sacrifice for sins forever, sat down at the right hand of God"*

(Hebrews 10:11-12).

Jesus has opened the way for all believers to come boldly before the Throne of God to receive His help in the time of need. In the holy of holies, deep within our heart—that place of absolute surrender before God—we offer to Him our most intimate expressions of worship. God receives our worship on the basis of Christ's blood and openly responds to us in, and through, His manifested love. The fellowship brought about by this level of worship cannot be expressed in words. It will only be evidenced by our level of surrender to His Lordship.

The pattern of worship that is established within the Tabernacle of Moses is eternal. The principles of approach to God, by way of the blood and the cleansing of the Word, still apply to us today. All of the requirements of the Law and the rituals of the sacrifices have been fulfilled in Jesus, and His sacrifice on the Cross.

The Tabernacle of Moses establishes a pattern of worship that flows out of redemption. We have been reconciled to God through the shed blood of Jesus. God has called us to minister before Him as kings and priests. Worship and ruler-ship is the desire of God for man.

Chapter Seven

WORSHIP IS OUR RESPONSE TO KNOWING GOD

The concept, that God would have a need of any kind, is very difficult for one to comprehend. The Bible clearly portrays God as being completely self-sufficient: He does not need a counselor or an advisor. He has no equal in all of heaven or earth. When God created the heavens and the earth, He didn't need anyone's help. God is the sum total of all knowledge and wisdom, both known and unknown to man; therefore, He does not need a teacher or a mentor. God is, in and of Himself, the sum total of all power; therefore, He never needs another source from which to obtain His power in order to function.

Though God is totally self-sufficient, He does have a need. This need is not a small or insignificant need; it is the consuming desire within God's heart. God revealed His need and desire when He created man. God needed and desired a source of responsive love to Him. He needed a higher source of response than that of the angels who served Him continually. God needed and wanted a family who would share willingly in all that He had to offer.

In the wisdom of His counsel, God created man in His own image. Man was created as a free moral agent and He was given the power of choice. As previously mentioned, man was to fellowship with God through his worship, and he was to rule over the works of God's hands.

As with all of God's creation, man was created for the pleasure of God. *"Thou art worthy, O Lord, to receive glory and honor and power: for Thou hast created all things, and for Thy pleasure they are and were created"* (Revelation 4:11). Man faithfully discharged his ministry of worship and ruler-ship, and the Lord received pleasure from him. God's need was for man to willingly, out of a heart of love and desire, respond to the myriad of daily expressions of love that God lavished on man.

God wanted more than just the response of service from man, for He already had that from the angels. God wanted man to respond to

Him in the same manner that He responded to man. God wanted man to respond to Him with loving fellowship, as is seen in friendship. He wanted man to recognize the greatness of the created works of His hands and offer to Him the fruit of his lips—praise. God wanted man to come before Him with intimate expressions of worship based on Who He is, not just what He has done. God wanted man to respond to Him much like a son responds to his father; a son appreciates and offers his gratitude to his father for all of his father's provisions. Out of a thankful heart, the son releases his love to his father simply for the presence of his person.

The Apostle John, under the inspiration of the Holy Spirit, penned three words that so completely describe God, and reveal God's need for man. The three words are found in I John 4:8, *"God is love."* It is so simple, yet, so profound. Love is not just what God does, love is what God is.

It is vitally important for us to understand that God has not just intellectually determined to love us; God is actually, emotionally involved with us. If God were merely intellectually involved with man, He would have destroyed man completely because of his rebellion and subsequent transgression of God's Law; and then He would have started over. With an intellectual love only, God would never have reached out in redemption and sent His only begotten Son to die on the Cross; thus, providing a ransom for man from his sins.

Love always creates a need within those who are in love. Love, when expressed, needs to be recognized and responded too. Also, love when expressed, needs to be received. Only a sincere response, from the one to whom the expression of love was given, will satisfy the heart of the lover.

The heart of God, and the heart of man, both have a vacuum within that heart that only the love of the other can fill. The vacuum within man's heart cannot be filled with power, wealth, knowledge, wisdom, pleasure, or popularity. There is nothing known to man that will fill or satisfy the vacuum within man's heart. Only by embracing God and His love, through the indwelling presence of the Holy Spirit, can the vacuum within the heart of man be filled and satisfied.

The vacuum within the heart of God cannot be filled or satisfied with empty rituals of loveless praise, shallow worship, or forced service. Only through the loving response of man's heart in praise, intimate worship, and willing service, can the vacuum in the heart of God be filled and satisfied.

> *"For many years we have been told of the God-shaped vacuum that is in the life of every person, and that none can be fully satisfied until that vacuum is filled with God. This is, of course, illustratively true. But how about the man-shaped vacuum in the heart of God? If God took part of Himself out to form man, it left a vacuum that only man can fill. When man returns to the heart of God in love—no longer as a child, but as a bride—it satisfies, completes, and fulfills God."*[3]

Love involves emotion. Whenever love and emotion are expressed a response is needed, and even demanded, from the object of the lover. Adam, before his act of rebellion, openly and freely responded to all of God's expressions of love to him. Adam and God were both completely fulfilled in each other's expressions and responses of love. From his heart, Adam returned to the heart of God his expressions of love through his fellowship and worship.

After Adam rebelled and sinned, his expressions of love, fellowship, and worship of God, ceased. The sin of Adam passed to every man; therefore, every man failed to understand the need within the heart of God. Failing to understand God's need for fellowship and worship, man was not responsive to God's overtures of love.

Due to sin, man soon lost his knowledge of God's great love and his desire for Him. Man viewed God as a distant and demanding taskmaster. Gone was the understanding of God's tender, loving nature, and His deep desire for fellowship through friendship and relationship. Man lost sight of his purpose in the earth to be a worshiper of God, and a ruler over God's creation.

---

[3] *Elements of Worship*, Copyright 1985 by Judson Cornwall, Bridge Publishing.

Due to sin, man's heart became as hard as stone and was incapable of receiving, or giving love as God intended. Man's spiritual eyes became blind to the truth and the rightness of God's ways, as well as, His love for him. Instead of treating God as a loving friend, man treated God, for the most part, as his enemy. He treated God as an enemy who looked for ways to rob man of his pleasures by oppressing him with narrow-minded standards for living.

Due to sin, man no longer breathed God's name in prayerful worship. Instead he often cursed God and took His name in vain. No longer did man reverence, embrace, or adore God's presence. Instead, he disdained and avoided God's presence in order to pursue the darkness of his wicked and rebellious heart.

Man was completely lost to God; therefore, he could not fulfill His divine purpose in the earth. Yet, God, in His unfathomable love, pursued the elusive and unregenerate heart of man. God intended to redeem man from his sins and restore man to his relationship with God and his purpose in the earth.

God established the way of approach for man to return to God and be restored to his purpose in the earth. He could only approach God through the blood of the sacrifice; wherein man could be redeemed and restored. God established patterns of worship for man to follow so that man would understand what God desired and wanted of him. Through these established patterns of worship, man could express his love to God and receive God's overwhelming response of love in return.

The only problem with this plan was that man had completely lost his understanding and knowledge of who God was and, therefore, what God wanted. So God set out to reveal Himself to man so that man could love Him again. God's revelation of Himself was progressive, primarily because He was dealing with man's fallen nature and limited understanding. Therefore, He revealed Himself to man a little at a time. With each increment of revelation of Himself to man, God then waited for man to live within that revelation and apply his new understanding.

God wanted man to really know Him. He wanted man to know Him by the heart and not just the head. He wanted man to know who He was, how He felt, and what He wanted and needed in a relationship. God wanted man to understand how he could fulfill his purpose in the earth and by doing so, fully please God. God knew that the only way man could ever really know Him was to know Him deep within the heart. The problem however, was that man's heart was as hard as stone and unable to receive, or respond to, God's love.

The Lord addressed the problem of the heart through the Prophet Jeremiah. Jeremiah tells us that God will take the heart of stone out of man; replacing it with a heart that is not only responsive to Him, but deeply desires to know Him as well. *"Then I will give them a heart to know Me, that I am the Lord; and they shall be My people, and I will be their God, for they shall return to Me with their whole heart"* (Jeremiah 24:7).

Creation is an indicator of God's desire for man to become personally acquainted with Him, for all of the attributes of God are evident in His creation. The testimony of God's greatness, and His love for man, are written within the works of His hands, *"For since the creation of the world His invisible attributes are clearly seen, being understood by the things that are made, even His eternal power and Godhead, so that they are without excuse"* (Romans 1:20). One has but to look at the beauty of the sun's rising, or its' setting on the horizon, to see the glory of God. Gazing at the majestic mountain peaks as they tower over the grassy meadows, tells us of the greatness of God. To stand on the shore of the sea and watch the moonlight dance on the water, stirs the heart with thoughts of God.

All of God's creation reveals to man that God made the earth for him; not only to inhabit, but to enjoy. *"The heavens declare the glory of God; and the firmament shows His handiwork"* (Psalms 19:1). God intends, as a result of man's enjoyment of the earth, for man to offer Him praise and worship. From out of the greatness of His creation, God speaks to the heart of man saying..."If you only knew Me, I know you would love Me and worship Me only."

Chapter Eight

WORSHIP REVEALED IN THE NAMES OF GOD

God continued in His progressive revelation of Himself to man through His name. The various aspects of God's name are much like a diamond that has many facets. God revealed Himself in capsules of truth that spoke of His nature, His attributes, and His desired relationship with man. God did not give a full revelation of Himself to Israel all at once; rather, He revealed one aspect at a time. As each revelation was embraced, and its truth was lived out in the hearts of the Israelites, God would give another revelation of Himself.

Each of the truths about God that were revealed in His name, were completely fulfilled in Jesus Christ. The Word teaches us that Jesus is the fullness of the Godhead lived out in the flesh. Therefore, in Jesus, we see the complete revelation of God as found in Colossians 1:19, *"For it pleased the Father that, in Him, all the fullness should dwell."* Jesus told His disciples that if they saw Him and were able to comprehend Him, they were actually seeing and comprehending God the Father. Jesus was God Himself, revealed in the flesh.

> *"In the beginning was the Word, and the Word was with God, and the Word was God. He was in the beginning with God. All things were made through Him, and without Him nothing was made that was made. In Him was life, and the life was the light of men. And the light shines in the darkness, and the darkness did not comprehend it. And the Word became flesh and dwelt among us, and we beheld His glory, the glory as of the only begotten of the Father, full of grace and truth"* (John 1:1-5, 14).

Moses asked God what he should tell the people when they asked him who had sent him. God told Moses to tell the people that "I AM THAT I AM," had sent him to them. *"And God said to*

Moses, 'I AM WHO I AM.' And He said, 'Thus you shall say to the children of Israel, 'I AM has sent me to you'" (Exodus 3:14). In this simple name, there was a deep and profound truth that spoke, not only to Israel, but to us as well. God was revealing to Moses and Israel that He was eternally in the "now" of their lives. What God was yesterday to their forefathers, He was to them today. What He is today, He will be tomorrow, and forevermore, *"For I am the Lord, I change not"* (Malachi 3:6).

God also instructed Moses to tell the people that He was the same faithful God who cut covenant with their forefathers, Abraham, Isaac, and Jacob. In other words, God revealed to Moses, and the children of Israel, that He was a covenant-keeping God. God knew that they would understand this, as cutting covenants was a common practice among the people. This was the strongest relationship known to man in the earth and God knew that they realized the seriousness of someone failing to keep the covenant that had been cut.

> *"Moreover God said to Moses, 'Thus you shall say to the children of Israel: "The Lord God of your fathers, the God of Abraham, the God of Isaac, and the God of Jacob, has sent me to you. This is My name forever, and this is My memorial to all generations"'"* (Exodus 3:15).

God wanted Israel to know that He would not fail in His end of the covenant that He had cut with Abraham, and that He would keep His Word to them—He wants us to know the same. Through His compound redemptive names, God reveals the redemptive work of Christ in our lives.

God revealed Himself as "JEHOVAH-TSIDKENU," which means, "JEHOVAH OUR RIGHTEOUSNESS." This name of God revealed to man that there would be a transaction of redemption that would take place that would completely restore man to God. Jesus became sin so that we could become the righteousness of God in Him. *"For He made Him who knew no sin to be sin for us, that we might become the righteousness of God in Him"* (II Corinthians 5:21).

Jesus was our substitute in death; thus, He paid our sin debt in full, and through His blood we receive total forgiveness for our sins. All of our sins—past, present, and future, are forgiven if we will come to Jesus and appropriate His blood to our hearts. *"If we confess our sins, He is faithful and just to forgive us our sins, and to cleanse us from all unrighteousness"* (I John 1:9).

Forgiven, we have been made righteous before God. Jesus is our righteousness. Through His redemptive name, "JEHOVAH TSIDKENU," God said to man..."If you really knew Me, I know you would love Me and worship Me only."

God revealed Himself as "JEHOVAH-M'KADDESH," which means, "JEHOVAH WHO SANCTIFIES." The word "sanctify" means to be set apart or to be separated. We are to be separated from the world and separated to God in holiness.

Through His death on the Cross, Jesus not only redeemed us from sin, He also delivered us from the power of sin. Sin is to have absolutely no dominion over any area of our life. Jesus, through His blood, has set us free from the slavery of sin to become the servants of God. *"But God be thanked that though you were slaves of sin, yet you obeyed from the heart that form of doctrine to which you were delivered. And having been set free from sin, you became slaves of righteousness"* (Romans 6:17-18).

Through His redemptive name, "JEHOVAH-M'KADDESH," God said to man..."If you only knew Me, I know you would love Me and worship Me only."

God revealed Himself as "JEHOVAH-SHALOM," which means, "JEHOVAH OUR PEACE." Our sin separated us from God; thus we were out of harmony with God and His purpose. Through the shed blood of Jesus, the barrier of sin that separated us from God was broken down. *"By Him to reconcile all things to Himself, by Him, whether things on earth or things in heaven, having made peace through the blood of His cross. And you, who once were alienated and enemies in your mind by wicked works, yet now He has reconciled"* (Colossians 1:20-21). Now we have peace with God, and have full access to the Father.

Not only does the blood of Jesus establish our peace with God, it also establishes us in the peace of God. No matter what circumstance we are faced with, the peace of God will keep our hearts at rest.

> *"Be anxious for nothing, but in everything by prayer and supplication, with thanksgiving, let your requests be made known to God; and the peace of God, which surpasses all understanding, will guard your hearts and minds through Christ Jesus"* (Philippians 4:6-7).

The peace of God that Jesus imparts to us is not fragile like the peace of the world. His peace is lasting and will make us strong in the face of adversity. *"Peace I leave with you, My peace I give to you; not as the world gives do I give to you. Let not your heart be troubled, neither let it be afraid"* (John 14:27).

Jesus is our Peace and we do not ever need to be afraid. He will not only guide us, but He will also keep us in His peace. Through His redemptive name, "JEHOVAH-SHALOM," God said to man..."If you only knew Me, I know that you would love Me and worship Me only."

God revealed Himself as "JEHOVAH-SHAMMAH," which means, "JEHOVAH IS PRESENT." There is never a time that we are separated from God's presence. It doesn't matter what our circumstance may be—God is always with us. It doesn't matter where we go in the earth—God is there.

The Psalmist David knew what it was to fall into hard times and feel lost in the midst of adverse circumstances. Yet, even with all of his problems, he knew that Jehovah-Shammah was always with him.

> *"Where can I go from Your Spirit? Or where can I flee from Your presence? If I ascend into heaven, You are there; If I make my bed in hell, behold, You are there. If I take the wings of the morning, and dwell in the uttermost parts of the sea, even there Your hand shall lead me, and Your right hand shall hold me"* (Psalms 139:7-10).

God is ever present with us because the Holy Spirit dwells within our hearts. Wherever we go, He goes with us; and whatever comes against us, He faces it with us. We must never take for granted the privilege of walking in the fullness of the presence of the Holy Spirit. Actually, being filled with the Holy Spirit is not an option to us—it is a command of God. *"And be not drunk with wine, wherein is excess; but be filled with the Spirit"* (Ephesians 5:18).

The presence of the Holy Spirit is absolutely essential if we are to fulfill our destiny in the earth. The Holy Spirit teaches us what we need to know about God and how we can serve Him effectively. Our power to be a witness for the Lord is only through the Holy Spirit's presence. In order to be the worshiper of God we are supposed to be, we must pursue holiness in our lives. The ministry of the Holy Spirit is to convict us of areas that need to be changed, and through the Word, He cleanses us from sin.

The Holy Spirit gives us the power to defeat the devil; however, we must put on the whole armor of Jesus, use the weapons of our warfare, and stand firmly rooted on God's Word. It is the ministry of the Holy Spirit to point us to Jesus. Through the guidance and the inspiration of the Holy Spirit, we offer to the Lord those expressions of praise and worship that will please the Father's heart.

What an overwhelming source of comfort and assurance to know that the Lord, by the Holy Spirit, will never leave us nor will He forsake us. Through His redemptive name "JEHOVAH-SHAMMAH," God said to man…"If you only knew Me, I know you would love Me and worship Me only."

God revealed Himself as "JEHOVAH-ROPHE," which means, "JEHOVAH HEALS." The word "rophe" means, "to restore, cure, or heal." This does not just apply to the physical arena; it also applies to the spiritual and moral aspects of our lives as well.

Jesus submitted Himself to the will of the Father by becoming the sacrifice for the sins of mankind. Through His death on the Cross, Jesus redeemed man from sin. Jesus also purchased healing for mankind by the stripes that were laid on His back, prior to dying on the Cross.

The Prophet Isaiah, under the inspiration of the Holy Spirit, looked down the corridors of time and saw the suffering of the Lord. He saw the stripes that were laid on His back and fully understood that they were for the healing of mankind; *"But He was wounded for our transgressions, He was bruised for our iniquities; the chastisement for our peace was upon Him, and by His stripes we are healed"* (Isaiah 53:5).

Jesus came to deliver man from the curse of the Law. This curse was manifested in man's life as poverty, sickness, and death. Jesus revealed to us how much God cares about our pain and sorrow. God is touched by what touches us and He forever cares about what is concerning us.

God proved His love toward us in sending Jesus to suffer in our place. Now through the stripes on Jesus' back, we can claim our healing by faith. God not only desires to heal us of our illnesses, He desires for us to walk in His divine health. *"Beloved, I wish above all things that thou mayest prosper and be in health, even as thy soul prospers"* (III John 2).

Through His redemptive name "JEHOVAH-ROPHE," God said to man..."If you only knew Me, I know you would love Me and worship Me only."

God revealed Himself as "JEHOVAH-JIREH," which means, "JEHOVAH'S PROVISION SHALL BE SEEN." Man, because of sin, was living under a curse of failure. This failure manifested in man's sickness, man's death, and man's poverty. Jesus came to deliver us from the curse of failure by becoming the curse, and suffering the fullness of the curse, for us. *"Christ has redeemed us from the curse of the law, having become a curse for us (for it is written, 'Cursed is everyone who hangs on a tree')"* (Galatians 3:13).

The Roman soldiers designed a crown of thorns and thrust it down into Jesus' brow. Thorns represent or symbolize the curse of Adam's failure in the Garden of Eden, and Adam's failure passed to all men. However, the blood of Jesus broke, and removed, the curse from man. We are absolutely free from failure in every area of our lives, including finances. God's Word teaches us, over and over again, that God desires to bless His people. *"He who did not spare His own Son, but delivered Him up for us all, how shall He not with Him also freely give us all things"* (Romans 8:32)?

Wherever there is a need, Jesus becomes our full provision and our continual source of supply. Jesus taught His disciples that the

Father knew each and every need that they had. He taught them that not only did the Father know their needs, but that the Father knew of their need before they even were aware that they had a need. The Father, in His love and desire to bless His people, made provision for those needs before they manifested. That full provision is in His Son, Jesus.

Jesus taught the disciples, that if they would put the Lord first in their hearts and in their pursuits in life, that all of their needs would be met by the Father's provision. Because He is Jehovah-Jireh, we never need to worry about our daily provisions, for in Him, they shall be provided. Through His redemptive name "JEHOVAH-JIREH," God said to man..."If you only knew Me, I know you would love Me and worship Me only."

God revealed Himself as "JEHOVAH-NISSI," which means, "JEHOVAH OUR BANNER." The word "banner" is translated as "pole, ensign, or standard." As an ensign, it was a signal to God's people to rally to Him when they were in battle and realize that He was their victory. Jesus has become our banner of victory for He has conquered and overcome all of the battles that the world brings against us. *"These things I have spoken to you, that in Me you may have peace. In the world you will have tribulation; but be of good cheer, I have overcome the world"* (John 16:33).

Jesus gives us His victory and makes us victorious conquerors. He broke sin's power through his death on the Cross. He abolished death, and the fear of death, through His resurrection. We do not need to fear death, for Jesus has removed the fear of death from the heart of the believer.

> *"Inasmuch then as the children have partaken of flesh and blood, He Himself likewise shared in the same, that through death He might destroy him who had the power of death, that is, the devil, and release those who through fear of death were all their lifetime subject to bondage"* (Hebrews 2:14-15).

Jesus is our victory in every battle of life, as well as, our victory over death. Through His name "JEHOVAH-NISSI," God said to man..."If you only knew Me, I know you would love Me and worship Me only."

God revealed Himself as "JEHOVAH-ROHI," which means, "JEHOVAH OUR SHEPHERD." The word "ro'eh" means to, "feed or to lead to pasture" as a shepherd does his flock. Jesus is our good shepherd Who cares for us and provides for us; and we are the sheep of His pasture.

> *"I am the good shepherd. The good shepherd gives His life for the sheep. My sheep hear My voice, and I know them, and they follow Me. And I give them eternal life, and they shall never perish; neither shall anyone snatch them out of My hand"* (John 10:11, 27-28).

Jesus calls each of us by our name as He leads us into the paths of God. The Word of the Lord teaches us that as righteous men, our steps are ordered and directed of the Lord. If we will learn to listen to His voice, we will know His direction for our lives.

Jesus will lead us through the valley of the shadow death when our earthly body yields to death. He will take us safely to our Father's house that has been prepared for us. There, with the Father, we will dwell for all of eternity. We will blend our voice with the hosts of heaven and offer our worship at the feet of the Lamb. The Psalmist David knew the Lord to be his Shepherd, his Provider, his Protector, and his Guide into eternity.

> *"The Lord is my shepherd; I shall not want. Yea, though I walk through the valley of the shadow of death, I will fear no evil; For You are with me; Your rod and Your staff, they comfort me. Surely goodness and mercy shall follow me all the days of my life; and I will dwell in the house of the Lord forever"* (Psalms 23:1, 4, 6).

Through His name "JEHOVAH-ROHI," God said to man..."If you only knew Me, I know you would love Me and worship Me only."

God has called every believer to worship Him in the power of the Holy Spirit according to the pattern set forth in His Word. This pattern of worship is founded upon our redemption from sin. From this foundation of redemption, God reveals Himself to us so that we have the choice to worship Him. Only as we come to really know God in our hearts, can we respond to Him in praise and worship. As we grow in our understanding of Him we will progressively, and with great desire, increase the intimacy of our worship of Him.

One day we will sweep through heaven's gates and will gather around the Throne of God. There we will see Jesus, the precious Lamb of God. We will see the imprint from the nails which scar His hands and His feet. We will see His side which was pierced; and His brow which carries the scars from the crown of thorns. Oh, the indescribable rapture of that first glimpse of Jesus, our Savior, and King. Our hearts will burst forth in songs of praise and worship to our God. Redemption's story will be our theme song throughout all of eternity.

> *"And they sang a new song, saying: 'You are worthy to take the scroll, and to open its seals; For You were slain, and have redeemed us to God by Your blood out of every tribe and tongue and people and nation, and have made us kings and priests to our God; and we shall reign on the earth'"* (Revelation 5:9-10).

BIBLIOGRAPHY

Editor: Alexander, David, *Eerdmans Handbook to the Bible*. Grand Rapids, Michigan: W. B. Eerdmans Publishing Co., 1973.

Allis, Oswald T., *God Spake by Moses*. Philadelphia, PA: The Presbyterian Reformed Publishing Co., 1951.

Ben-Gurion, David, *The Jews In Their Land*. Garden City, New York: Doubleday & Company, 1974.

Bonhoeffer, Dietrich, *Creation and Fall: Temptation*. New York, New York: McMillan Publishing Co., Inc., 1959.

Editor: Buttrick, George Arthur. *The Interpreter's Dictionary of the Bible/K-Q*. Nashville/New York: Abindgon Press, 1962.

Conner, Kevin J., *The Foundations of Christian Doctrine*. Portland Oregon: Bible Temple Publications, 1980.

Conner, Kevin J., *The Tabernacle of Moses*. Portland Oregon: The Center Press, 1974.

Conner, Kevin and Malmin, Ken, *The Covenants*. Portland, Oregon: Bible Temple Publications, 1983.

Cornwall, Judson, *David Worshiped A Living God*. Shippensburg, Pennsylvania: Destiny Image Publishers, 1989.

Cornwall, Judson, *The Secret of Personal Prayer*. Altamonte Springs, Florida: Creation House: Strang Communications, 1988.

Cornwall, Judson, *Meeting God*. Altamonte Springs, Florida: Creation House: Strang Communications, 1986.

Cornwall, Judson, *Elements of Worship*. Plainfield, New Jersey: Bridge Publishing, Inc., 1985.

Cornwall, Judson, *Let Us Worship*. Plainfield, New Jersey: Bridge Publishing, Inc., 1983.

Cornwall, Judson, *Let Us Be Holy*. Plainfield, New Jersey: Logos International, 1978.

Cornwall, Judson, *Let Us Praise*. Plainfield, New Jersey: Logos International, 1973.

DeHaan, M.R. (M.D.), *The Tabernacle*. Grand Rapids, Michigan: Zondervan Publishing House, 1966.

Evans, William, *The Great Doctrines of the Bible*. Chicago, Illinois: The Moody Bible Institute of Chicago, 1974.

Exell, Joseph S., *The Biblical Illustrator/Romans I*. Grand Rapids, Michigan: Baker Book House, 1967.

Editor: Gardner, Joseph L. Principal adviser and editorial consultant: Frank, Harry Thomas., *Readers Digest Atlas of the Bible*. Pleasantville, New York: The Readers' Digest Assoc., Inc., 1981.

Hayford, Jack W., *Worship His Majesty*. Dallas, Texas: Word Publishing, 1987.

Holy Bible, Authorized King James Version. Nashville, Tennessee: Thomas Nelson, Inc., 1975.

Ironside, H.A., *Lectures on the Levitical Offerings*. Neptune, New Jersey: Loizeaux Brothers.

Josephus, Flavius, *The Works of Josephus*. Peabody, Massachusetts: Hendrickson Publishers, 1987.

Keil, C.F. (D.D.) and Delitzsch, F. (D.D.), *Commentaries on the Old Testament/The Pentateuch Vol. I*. Grand Rapids, Michigan: W. B. Eerdmans Publishing Co., 1971.

Keil, C.F. (D.D.) and Delitzsch, F. (D.D.), *Commentaries on the Old Testament/The Pentateuch Vol. II*. Grand Rapids, Michigan: W. B. Eerdmans Publishing Co., 1971.

Kenyon, E.W., *The Father And His Family*. Lynnwood, Washington: Kenyon's Gospel Publishing Society, 1964.

Ketcherside, Carl W., *The Royal Priesthood*. St. Louis, Missouri: Mission Messenger, 1956.

Livingston, G. Herbert, *The Pentateuch in Its Cultural Environment*. Grand Rapids, Michigan: Baker Book House, 1974.

Lloyd-Jones, D. Martin, *Romans: Assurance*. Grand Rapids, Michigan: Zondervan Publishing House, 1972.

Lloyd-Jones, D. Martin, *Romans/The Law: Its Functions and Limits*. Grand Rapids, Michigan: Zondervan Publishing House, 1974.

Plaut, Gunther W., *The Torah/A Modern Commentary*. New York, New York: Union of American Hebrew Congregations, 1981.

Pratney, W.A., *The Nature and Character of God*. Minneapolis, Minnesota: Bethany House Publishers, 1988.

Schultz, Samuel J., *The Old Testament Speaks*. New York, New York: Harper & Row, Publishers, 1960.

Simpson, A.B., *Christ in the Tabernacle*. Harrisburg, Pennsylvania: Christian Publications, Inc.

Smith, William (L.L.D.), *Smith's Bible Dictionary*. Nashville: Thomas Nelson Publishers, 1979.

Soltau, Henry W., *The Holy Vessels and Furniture of the Tabernacle*. Grand Rapids, Michigan: Kregel Publications, 1973.

Soltau, Henry W., *The Tabernacle/The Priesthood and the Offerings*. Grand Rapids, Michigan: Kregel Publications, 1972.

Strong, James, *Strong's Exhaustive Concordance*. Marshaltown, Delaware: The National Foundation for Christian Education.

Tozer, A.W., *Whatever Happened to Worship?* (Compiled by G. B. Smith), Camp Hill, Pennsylvania: Christian Publications, 1985.

Tozer, A.W., *Man: The Dwelling Place of God*. Harrisburg, Pennsylvania: Christian Publications, Inc., 1966.

Wuest, Ken S., *Wuest's Word Studies/Romans*. Grand Rapids, Michigan: W. B. Eerdmans Publishing Co., 1976.

www.ingramcontent.com/pod-product-compliance
Lightning Source LLC
Chambersburg PA
CBHW051710040426
42446CB00008B/808